Simple Transitions for Infants and Toddlers

by Karen Miller

Acknowledgments

All books take shape as the result of an author's exposure to the ideas and talents of many people. I wish I could acknowledge personally the hundreds of childcare teachers who are in my mind from the over 30 years I have spent observing and learning from them. And then there are the countless dedicated infant and toddler teachers, administrators, and trainers who have generously shared ideas and insights at professional conferences and training workshops around the country. It is this professional caring and sharing that has made our field dynamic and ever-improving. Specifically, I would like to thank Leah Curry-Rood for helping me to conceptualize this book and brainstorm its initial outline, as well as providing the various lists of children's books provided in the content. Finally, the magic touch and hard work of a good editor, in this case Kate Kuhn, make a book come together effectively. Thank you, all of you!

Dedication

This book is dedicated, with respect and admiration, to infant and toddler teachers everywhere. Your influence is tremendous.

Simple
TRANSITIONS

for Infants and Toddlers

Karen Miller

Illustrations: Marie Ferrante Doyle
Photographs: Mary Duru

gryphon house, ® Inc.
Beltsville, Maryland

Copyright

Published by Gryphon House, Inc.
10726 Tucker Street, Beltsville, MD 20705
301.595.9500; 301.595.0051 (fax); 800.638.0928 (toll-free)

Visit us on the web at www.gryphonhouse.com

Cover art: Comstock Images, www.comstock.com

Library of Congress Cataloging-in-Publication Information

Miller, Karen.
  Simple transitions for infants and toddlers / by Karen Miller. p. cm.
  Includes bibliographical references and index.
  ISBN13: 978-0-87659-298-4
  ISBN10: 0-87659-298-1
 1. Child care. 2. Infants--Care. 3. Toddlers--Care. 4. Child care services. I. Title.
  HQ778.5.M55 2005
  362.71'2--dc22   2004022104

Bulk purchase

Gryphon House books are available for special premiums and sales promotions as well as for fund-raising use. Special editions or book excerpts also can be created to specification. For details, contact the Director of Marketing at Gryphon House.

Disclaimer

Gryphon House, Inc. and the author cannot be held responsible for damage, mishap, or injury incurred during the use of or because of activities in this book. Appropriate and reasonable caution and adult supervision of children involved in activities and corresponding to the age and capability of each child involved, is recommended at all times. Do not leave children unattended at any time. Observe safety and caution at all times.

Every effort has been made to locate copyright and permission information.

Table of Contents

Introduction 7

Chapter 1: General Principles and Techniques 11

Develop Consistency in the Daily Flow of Activities 11
Invent and Use Rituals .12
Make Your Classroom Space Work for You 12
Tell Children What's Going to Happen Next 12
Offer Rehearsals 13
Create Nonverbal Signals 13
Use a Pet Puppet 13
Entice Rather Than Command 14
Just Do It 14
Match Children's Development 15
Help Children Re-Enter the Group 15

Chapter 2: Center Transitions 17

Entering Childcare 17
Primary Caregivers 22
Continuity of Care 23
The Hardest Transition—Moving From the Infant Room
    to the Toddler Room 24
Moving from the Toddler Room to Preschool 27
Transitions When a Child Leaves the Program 28
Staff Transitions 29
Staff Changes 30
Weekend-to-Monday Transition 31

Chapter 3: Daily Transitions With Infants 33

Individualize Schedules .33
Morning Separation From Parent 35
Transitions Throughout the Day 39
Diapering 42
Playtime 43
Some Developmental Transitions 48
Going Outside 50
Sleeping 52
Pick-Up Time 55
When the Child's Routine Changes 57

Chapter 4: Daily Transitions With Toddlers 59

Morning Separation 60
Transitional Objects 68
Establishing the Daily Schedule 72
Morning Gathering Time 73
Snack Time 75
The Transition Into Playtime 77
Play Entry Skills 79
Toddler Friendships 82
Moving From One Play Activity to Another 86
Sharing and Taking Turns 86
Cleanup Time 92
Circle Time 95
Story Time 97
Diapering 100
Toilet Learning 102
Outside Time 105
Hand Washing 110
Lunchtime 112
Transition From Lunch to Nap 115
Nap Time 116
The Afternoon 120
Behavior Transitions 121
Dealing With Tantrums 123
Bad-Weather Activities 124
End of the Day 126
Reunions With Parents 128

Chapter 5: Staff Training for Successful Transitions 133

Personalize 133
Nonverbal Communication 133
Feding Infants 134
Rituals 134
Late Afternoon or Bad Weather Fun 135
The Problem Hat Game 135
Learning Transtion Songs .135

Appendix 137

Developmental Notes 138
How to Set Up a Positive Learning Environment 148
Setting Up the Outdoor Environment 153
Recommended Books 157

Index 161

Introduction

When I told a professional friend that I was writing a book about transitions with infants and toddlers, she said, "Simple! Transitions: as few as possible. End of book!" Of course, she is right! However, I do think there is more to say on this topic.

Because the topics covered in this book usually are not addressed in early childhood education classes, new teachers often struggle to make it through the day and sometimes end up exhausted and discouraged. Yet, it doesn't have to be this way. The ideas and strategies in this book came from many years of observing real caregivers in hundreds of childcare settings who had developed the knack of moving smoothly through the day with contented infants and relatively cooperative toddlers. For the purposes of this book an infant is from birth to 18 months of age. A toddler, one who is up and "toddling," is from 13 months to three years of age. Yes, there is an overlap. This is to allow for individual differences in maturation.

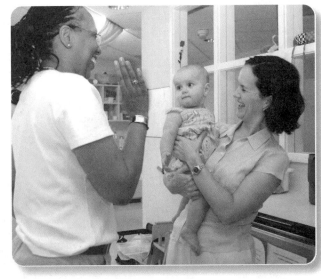

In the context of childcare, the word *transitions* implies the "in-between" times, moving from one part of the daily routine to another throughout the day. This book is really about helping children handle themselves in time and space, so that they know what to expect and what is expected of them. This book is also about helping children learn to deal with new situations, such as entering childcare for the first time or making the transition from the infant room to the toddler room.

Even when a child is cared for at home, not in a childcare center, transitions can be a challenge, as any parent who has tried to get a toddler out of the house in the morning can tell you. It takes effort and finesse to get toddlers to stop doing one thing and start doing something else, especially to conform to an adult's agenda. In a childcare setting, the caregiver must be conscious of the whole group. It takes teamwork with other staff, deciding ahead of time, and sometimes on the spot, who will be stationed where to support children while their partner gets something else done. Once beyond the infant room where most actions are individualized, transitions become major social activities. Toddlers move "en masse." Young children become conscious of each other as they gather or start something new. They are learning about getting things done.

Transitions make up a major portion of the real curriculum in infant and toddler child care. Infant and toddler teachers may feel that they don't have time for curriculum, viewing "curriculum" as special, planned learning activities. However, children often gain the most from what happens in everyday routines. We know that there are learning opportunities in virtually everything we do with these youngest children. Certainly, children's vocabularies grow as they learn the meaning of the words you speak. Children gain self-confidence and self-esteem as they find out what is expected of them and start to function independently. They come to "know the ropes" and develop a sense of belonging. How adults treat children, consistently, from day to day, has perhaps the largest impact on their healthy growth and development.

Life is full of transitions. We move from one developmental stage to another, in and out of relationships, from dependence to independence. We go from being the oldest in one school to the youngest in another. We enter the job market and change jobs. We move. How we handle both the large and the small transitions in our lives has a great impact on our general success in life. Is our ability to deal with life's transitions anchored in early childhood? Everything else seems to be, so it is likely that our earliest experiences with transitions influence how we will deal with change.

The truth is, transitions are hard! Any transition in life is challenging. We hang on to the old, and feel uncertain about the new. After the transition is made, we may question if we did the right thing. Narrow this down for very young children. Small daily transitions feel quite large to them. Their lives are small; therefore, the segments within seem big.

I hope this book helps you live in the moment with the infants and toddlers in your care. Slow down. Give them the time they need. Every moment has value. While you must keep the day moving and get things done, try to let go of the rush. Get out of the mindset of getting them ready for the next activity, the next stage, "the next life," and enjoy the wonder in front of you. Enjoy the NOW.

How to Use This Book

Although it is not necessary to read this book from cover to cover, it is important to read "General Principles and Techniques" (see Chapter 1, pages 11-15) and "Developmental Notes" (see Appendix page 138) before trying the transition ideas in the book. It is essential to have appropriate expectations for children in this age group. Certain principles and techniques make many situations go more smoothly. An understanding of these techniques, as well as where infants and toddlers are on the developmental spectrum, will make the advice in the rest of the book make even better sense.

After reading these sections, turn to the chapter or the particular daily transition that you find challenging. Pick and choose from the ideas and activities in this book that address your current needs. Try different things to discover what works best in your situation. Undoubtedly, you will come up with many variations of your own. Every childcare center and every group of children is different. Caregivers will constantly adjust and "tweak" the routine of the day to accommodate the children in the group. Variations in age and energy level will determine how you handle your daily routines.

This book includes transitions using different songs. Don't worry too much about the melody of the songs. Adjust the tunes and the words any way you wish. Make these songs your own, and make up your own.

With good planning, an understanding of the age of the child, and a few good techniques and activities up your sleeve, the days will go smoothly for you, the children, and parents, and everyone can get maximum benefit from your program.

SIMPLE TRANSITIONS FOR INFANTS AND TODDLERS

General Principles and Techniques

This chapter offers some basic transition techniques that apply in most situations. Keep them in mind when planning activities and routines. More discussion and specific examples of these principles appear throughout the book.

Develop Consistency in the Daily Flow of Activities

One of the best things you can do for yourself and the children in your care is to develop a basic, daily routine and stick to it. This is especially important in toddler rooms. Infants, on the other hand, benefit more from individualized, "demand" schedules. However, even in infant programs, you can establish a daily routine that forms the framework of your day. After a few days, the children learn this order. With consistency from day to day, they know what to expect. This gives children a sense of security and control. It makes transition times so much easier because the children, perhaps in order to demonstrate that they "know the ropes of this place," often automatically prepare to do the next thing. For instance, if you read books to the children in the Cozy Corner after snack every day, the children will begin to gather in the Cozy Corner without being told, as you help others finish their snacks.

This does not mean that you cannot vary what you do within segments of your daily schedule. Just remember that infants and toddlers like to do the same things over and over again, and they will look for the familiar.

Invent and Use Rituals

Rituals are specific ways of doing things that don't vary from day to day. For instance, you might sing the same lullaby at rest time, or always place an infant in a certain chair when it's time to eat. You might bring a certain puppet out to greet children at the beginning of the day, or always begin story time by singing a particular song. See how many of these mini-rituals you can develop for various segments of the day. Just as consistency in your daily routine helps children relax and feel in control, knowing what will happen and what is expected of them in many small parts of the day will help them be cooperative.

Make Your Classroom Space Work for You

Infants and toddlers orient themselves in space according to where certain objects are in the environment. For example, they may know they can find their favorite red truck on the shelf by the green rug. This is not to say that you should never rearrange the furniture, but do it only when there is a good reason. Have a "place for everything and everything in its place" as much as possible. Again, this gives very young children a sense of mastery and helps them to feel comfortable in the classroom, which, in turn, leads them to a greater sense of independence.

Tell Children What Is Going to Happen Next

No one likes abrupt change, especially when deeply involved in an activity. It is a courtesy to children to let them know what is going to happen next. Even babies can get the sense of this. *"Soon we will put the toys away and get ready to go outside."* If it happens every day, the children might even start the transition immediately. And even if they don't, resistance to the transition will likely be less.

Offer Rehearsals

When you're going to do something new, it's a good idea to have a rehearsal, to walk the children through the procedure, so they can know what to expect. Are you going to take the children on their first neighborhood walk, using a walking rope? First, let them practice holding onto knots in the rope while walking around the room or the playground. Will a child be moving to a new classroom? Many visits to the new classroom beforehand make it easier for the child when the transition occurs.

Create Nonverbal Signals

Use as many nonverbal signals as possible to prepare children for new segments of the day. Remember that language is not yet their primary way of figuring out their world. Find things that don't use words to signal your routines. For example, bring out a puppet to signal story time, or play a certain song or melody to signal cleanup time. When you dim the lights, children know it is time to rest. When you start slapping your knees in a certain rhythm as you walk around outside, children know it is time to go back inside.

Use words along with these nonverbal signals. In this way, children will receive the same message in a few different ways. Each message reinforces the other. Children even find it "fun" to comply with the nonverbal signals—it is almost like using a code.

Use a Pet Puppet

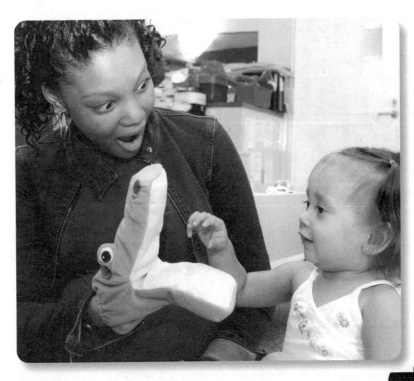

Although many people work with young children successfully without using a pet puppet, don't deprive yourself of this valuable aid. Children of all ages are drawn to a puppet and are eager to cooperate with it.

A "pet puppet" is different from other puppets that you might have in the classroom for children to use. You are the only one who manipulates the pet puppet. When you are finished using the pet puppet, put it away in its "house."

Do this so that you maintain the puppet's voice, personality, and influence. You will not be putting on "puppet shows" with this puppet. Pet puppets come out to talk informally with the children, listen to them, give hugs, and so on.

A pet puppet can be any kind of puppet, purchased or homemade. A fairly large hand puppet with a mouth that opens and closes so it can "talk" is best. But a puppet with arms that can grasp things is good, too. Your pet puppet should have a name, a special voice, a personality, and a decorated house or bed that sits on a high shelf. Some pet puppets are shy and quiet; some are curious and full of questions; some are quirky and mischievous; some are very sleepy and yawn all the time. Pet puppets are mentioned in several places in this book. Don't feel limited by these examples. Think of other times your puppet can show up and help.

Entice Rather Than Command

Often, young children are resistant to commands, or even requests phrased nicely. Present ideas and activities in a way that children are drawn to them. Phrases that are more likely to elicit cooperation from infants and toddlers include the following:

- "I have a great idea! Let's…"
- "I think it would be fun to…"
- "How about we…"
- "I know! We could…"

Just Do It

Sometimes called "flop and do," this well-used and popular transition technique means simply to flop down on the floor and start doing something. This is an effective way to pull toddlers over to you and into the next activity. Nothing is as enticing to infants and toddlers as an adult on the floor.

Match Children's Development

The surest way to gain a child's interest and cooperation is to design an activity that exercises a new skill the child is working on. Infants and toddlers are such natural learners that they invent ways to practice new skills over and over again. Think about a toddler learning to climb. The child will climb everything available, safe or not. So, design many varied and safe ways for the child to climb. Conversely, if you expect a child to do something they are not developmentally ready for, such as to sit and listen for a long period of time, you will be met with lots of resistance. Therefore, know what you can expect from the age of the child generally, and get a feel for each child's specific interests and capabilities. Build on that knowledge.

Help Children Re-Enter the Group

One transition we rarely think about is how to get a child who has been removed from the group back into the classroom and playing peacefully with other children again. The discipline strategy of time out doesn't work well with toddlers because they have such a vague concept of time and are not good at abstract thinking. They cannot imagine what the outcome would have been had they behaved differently. It is much more effective to correct the situation on the spot and show the child how to act differently. Help the child succeed in interacting with the other children successfully so that everyone is pleased with the outcome.

Nevertheless, sometimes a child might be aware of your displeasure, such as when she has purposely hurt another child. Tempers are high and the room has an emotional charge. It is important not to leave the room in this state of tension. You have to establish a rapport again with the child. If a child believes she has done something wrong and cannot repair the situation, then she may continue to misbehave to punish both herself and you.

The best way to get back on good terms is to play with the child one on one. Find something to do that is totally different from what the child was involved in when the situation arose. Sensory play is often a very good choice because it is soothing. Then parallel play with the child, following the child's lead. This tells the child that you still like her. Gradually, you can involve other children, reinforcing peaceful play and commenting positively as the children interact with each other.

These techniques involve being respectful of who children are and what they can do, building on positives. Use these techniques and principles and your own common sense. Watch the children's reactions. Be consistent. Praise them for cooperation.

SIMPLE TRANSITIONS FOR INFANTS AND TODDLERS

Center Transitions

This chapter addresses the broader transitions a child makes over longer periods of time within a childcare center—entering childcare for the first time, changing rooms, moving into the toddler program, moving up to preschool, and changing teachers.

Entering Childcare

Moving from the sheltered environment of home and the loving care of a parent to being one of a group of children cared for by trained professionals is a major life transition for children and parents alike. An important goal of infant and toddler childcare providers is to make this entry into the wider world as smooth as possible. The words "loving care" (or the equivalent) are found somewhere in the mottos or mission statements of most high-quality childcare providers. Caregivers are taught to be responsive to infants and to make the environment as "home-like" as possible, which boils down to treating every child with empathy and respect.

Intake Interview

The time you spend with parents when they are deciding to enroll their child is your first opportunity to make a good impression and form a mutually respectful and friendly relationship. Both administrative staff and caregiving staff should be involved in this process. Administrators can explain things such as fees and payment processes, the yearly calendar, and various other policies and procedures. The caregiver should be there to discuss the specifics of care for the child. Now is a good time to introduce the idea of gradual enrollment to parents (see page 19).

The intake interview serves two purposes: to get information and to give information. It's probably best to start by finding out about the child and the family in front of you. The enrollment form for the childcare center will guide you. When you are finished with the essentials, invite the parents to ask questions.

- **Realize that silence doesn't mean complacency.** Don't assume that just because prospective parents are quiet they feel comfortable with everything.

- **Ask open-ended questions.** *"Is there anything you wonder about?"* is a good question.

- **Be inquisitive.** Prepare some questions to ask the parents to indicate that you are genuinely interested in their child. *"What are some of your child's favorite activities?" "How does your child let you know when she is upset?" "Tell me what you hope for your child in this childcare environment."*

- **Be willing to bend.** Stress that you know that every child is a precious individual and that you are flexible and willing to do things "their way" whenever possible.

- **Tell them about your program.** Describe a typical day, some of the activities you do with the children, and the names and interests of other staff members.

- **Wear your nametag and a smile.** Also, use the parents' names when you address them.

- **Interview parents in a special place.** Certainly, you want parents to see the classroom, however, it's best to conduct intake interviews in another area, away from the room where the children may distract you from the conversation. Parents need your full attention, and you need theirs. Create a comfortable setting for this purpose—not the staff lounge where tired caregivers come in to "flop."

- **Offer coffee or tea.**

- **Use photo albums.** A picture is worth a thousand words. Parents can quickly get a feel for the scope of your program through photos.

Using the Gradual Enrollment Process

If possible, it is wise to gradually increase the hours of a child's attendance over the first week or two of enrollment. Both children and parents seem to adjust more easily when the transition into childcare is gradual. Start with just an hour's visit with the parent present. Then suggest that the parent leave for a brief amount of time, come back, and spend more time in the classroom with the child. Finally, increase the visit to half a day, with the parent leaving for longer and longer periods of time, eventually leaving the child for the whole day. The timing of this will depend on each child's adjustment.

Welcoming the New Family

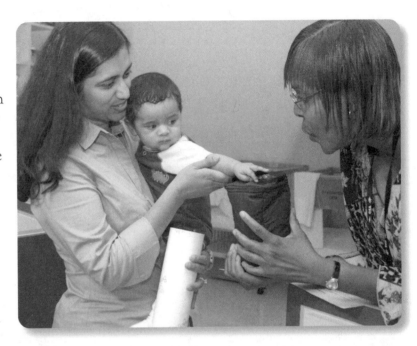

Once the family has chosen your center, make it apparent that you are happy to have the new family in your center. Inform staff that a new child will be entering the class, and provide them with the names of the parents, child, and any other information that will help staff welcome them wholeheartedly. Parents appreciate knowing that they and their child are important to everyone in the program. Let all staff know that a new family will be arriving. Encourage other caregivers to introduce themselves when they see the new family members and offer to be helpful in any way.

- 🐾 **Use your newsletter.** Introduce the family in your center's newsletter or classroom newsletter, if you have one.

- 🐾 **Highlight the family on your parent board.** A digital photo or instant camera can be helpful.

- 🐾 **Label the child's cubby ahead of time.** Also label any other spaces ahead of time, such as where diapers are kept and where food should be stored.

Empathizing With Parents

Most parents who make the decision to enroll their child in a childcare center have done much soul-searching, probably with the help (or not) of other parents, grandparents, and friends. *"How can you even think of leaving that baby?"* Parents may have heard this question from others, or asked it of themselves. Therefore, it is important for caregivers to empathize with what the parent is feeling and, above all, not to judge. That way, they can give maximum support to the parents by doing a good job with their child and communicating openly and often with the parents about how their child is benefiting from this childcare situation. Parents must feel that their child will benefit from being in your care without feeling inadequate about themselves. Share with them what you do each day and how daily activities and routines promote the healthy development of their child.

A certain level of grief is something almost all parents feel upon leaving their baby for the first time. They are fighting a basic instinct—to care for one's young. Some parents have mixed feelings. They are stressed about leaving their baby but may be eager to get back into the adult world. Others may experience a range of reactions from being totally comfortable to feeling anxious all the time. It is important to try to determine where each parent is on this spectrum and support them appropriately.

It is not uncommon for parents to feel competitive with the child's caregivers, although they may not even be aware of it. One fear is that the child will forget who his mother or father is and become more attached to the caregiver. Parents may feel that by enrolling their child in a center, they are "losing their baby." Many children do things unintentionally to reinforce this fear. For example, a child may call a caregiver "mommy," cry when the parent appears to pick him up, or run away from the parent.

Some parents feel badly if the child does not cry in the morning when he is dropped off. Explain to the parent that when the child calls you "mommy" it does not mean he doesn't know who his mother is. "Mommy" may simply be the toddler's generic term for women who take care of him. The crying at pick-up time is most likely a release of tension and a feeling of safety on the part of the child. See page 56 for a discussion of this phenomenon.

Building Rapport With the Parent

First, let parents get to know you so that you feel less like strangers to each other. Strongly urge parents to visit your classroom before their child starts attending regularly. An hour or two or half a day are best, rather than just a quick peek. Let them watch you perform the tasks of the day and interact with the children. This builds their confidence. Give parents a comfortable place to sit and let them know they can ask you questions at any time. This can be done with or without their child present.

- **Create a handout.** Write a brief description of your day that parents can have with them while they observe. You might explain why you take longer than necessary when changing a diaper, the hand-washing procedure you follow to maintain hygiene, how you individualize the program for each child, what your role is when you supervise the children's play, why it is your policy to go outside each day, and so on. In addition, if you feel it won't disrupt what you are doing with children, explain to parents what you are doing as you go through the day's activities.

All About Us

Materials
digital camera (or regular camera)   binder
paper   printer or copier

To Do
Take photos of caregivers during all the regular routines of the day. Place these in order and write a brief description for each photo. At the back of the book, have a photo of all staff who work in the program with a paragraph or two about each person. Print out a copy for new parents and let them take it home and keep it, or if using regular photos, put the pictures in a photo album and ask parents to take it home for a few days and then return it.

Parents appreciate these efforts to familiarize them with staff and the flow of the day. They can show it to grandparents and other members of the family. It also communicates that you are confident and proud of the work that you do with children.

Caregiver Biography (The Story of You)

A childcare center's enrollment forms are usually quite thorough. By the time parents complete all of the paperwork, they may feel that you know everything about them. Give parents the same advantage by creating an upbeat biography about yourself.

Materials
photograph of you
copier
paper

To Do
Get a good picture of yourself at work (use a photograph in which you are smiling). Then write several paragraphs about yourself. Focus on why you like working with infants or toddlers, your education and training, and your experience working with children. You might describe your family, pets, and hobbies, or anything else you think may be interesting to parents.

Make a copy for parents to keep, or include a copy in the book about your classroom (see activity on the previous page). Display this on your parent bulletin board near the entrance of your room so that any prospective parents can glance at it, as well. This is another way to help parents feel confident in the care you provide to their child.

Note: Helping the child adjust to the new situation is discussed in the Daily Transitions chapters for each age.

Early Communications

Plan to communicate with the new parents often during the first few weeks their child is enrolled.

- **Call them.** Offer to call the parent at work at a convenient time during the day and let him or her know how the child is doing.

- **Accept calls.** It might be more convenient for the parents to call you. Let them know that they are welcome to call, and tell them the best times to reach you.

- **Write notes.** You probably have some version of "What We Did Today" notes that you fill out for all the parents summarizing the child's diapering, eating, and sleeping, as well as the activities each child enjoyed. Fill these out and add some notes every now and then. Offer more elaborate descriptions of how the child responded to new activities.

- **Use photos.** A picture of their child happy, in the company of other children, can be very reassuring to parents.

- **Touch base.** At least once a week for about six weeks, have a brief "check-in" time with parents, just to see how they are feeling about things. This is not a formal conference; therefore, you may discuss issues over the phone if that is easier.

Primary Caregivers

It is good practice to assign each infant or toddler to a particular caregiver—someone who becomes an expert on that child. Each caregiver will end up with a small number of children for which he or she is primarily responsible. The primary caregiver comforts the child when the child is distressed, diapers and feeds the child, and tucks the child in at nap time (at least at first). That is not to say that no other staff person can diaper, feed, or comfort the child. Very quickly, most children become comfortable with all of the regular adults they see during the day. But it is the primary caregiver who should do most of the communicating with the parents about the child's adjustment and development. This is the person who does careful observations of the child, keeps notes on the child's progress, and makes educational plans for the child.

The main reason for primary caregivers is that children adjust more easily if there is one person to whom they can go when in distress— someone who is special and will support them. Although it is not exactly "bonding," it may be called an "emotional friendship." The primary caregiver is especially important for infants, who are learning to trust in the world. When children experience this basic trust, they can relax, venture out, feel safe, and benefit from the experiences offered to them. Without this trust, they will remain tense, "on guard," and less able to learn.

Primary caregivers also offer great benefits to parents. It makes things easier for a parent to have one individual with whom to communicate about his or her child. One of the primary caregiver's most important jobs is to get to know the parents well and encourage them to ask questions and raise concerns.

Continuity of Care

Continuity of care is the practice of moving the caregiver with the children as they develop, for two or even three years. To accomplish this, the center must establish primary caregivers for children. A caregiver starts out with a group of infants, then moves with the children to the toddler room, and then to the two-year-olds' room. When the children become preschoolers, generally the caregiver starts over with a new group of infants in the infant room.

Continuity of care does pose administrative challenges. Children and caregivers come and go. The child/staff ratio changes with toddlers and twos (at which time you can add extra children from the waiting list). However, acknowledging the benefits for children, many programs practice a modified form of continuity of care that seems to work very well. They move up one caregiver in the room with the children and someone else stays behind in the infant room for continuity with the children who remain. There may be "anchor staff" in the infant room and the toddler room—people who stay in that particular environment and are essentially in charge of the room, especially in orienting new staff, while other caregivers move up with the children.

At first, staff may resist implementing this practice. Many caregivers have a strong preference for working with a particular age group. All stages of infancy and toddlerhood are fascinating and there are strategies that help staff become effective caregivers for children of every age. With proper training and coaching, caregivers learn that the continuity of care system helps them develop stronger relationships with families, which is so critical in providing quality infant and toddler care. It also adds variety to their job. They are not doing the same thing day after day, year after year. Most of all, these caregivers get to see the results of their fine caregiving, by watching as "their babies" develop into competent preschoolers.

The Hardest Transition—Moving From the Infant Room to the Toddler Room

Moving from the infant room to the toddler room is so significant that it could be listed as a "life transition." It is the first of many times that an individual goes from being the oldest in the group to the youngest. While it signifies development and progress and should be a cause for pride as the child faces the adventures ahead, often it does not feel that way to parents. Once again, it can be the parents who suffer the most during this transition. Parents will need a lot of support and reassurance from the caregiving staff during this time. Parents have come to feel trust and comfort in the sheltered environment of the infant room. The toddler room may appear to be chaotic and noisy. Their child may seem small and vulnerable. They may fear that their child will be harmed.

🐾 **Explain how toddlers are active and impulsive in their exploration of the world around them.** The room may look messy at times because toddlers carry things around with them, drop them, and go to whatever else grabs their interest. Taking things away from other children, screaming in protest, and even a certain amount of physical assertion are to be expected at this age. And yes, every child will develop these behaviors to some degree, if they have not already demonstrated them.

- **Explain how you respond.** Describe to parents the steps you take to assure their child's close supervision and safety. For example, discuss using small groups, supervision techniques, and lots of coaching to help children learn how to play together.

- **Highlight advantages.** Point out to the parents how the child will benefit from a more stimulating environment and all of the new educational and social activities.

- **Empathize.** Emotionally, some parents feel that they are "losing their baby" at this step. They already see that their once cuddly infant is now pushing away, eager to explore the wider world. There is a certain finality in leaving the infant room.

- **Celebrate development.** Help parents take pride in the progress the child has made. Help them learn that a toddler is a wonderful thing to be.

- **Be a friend.** In classrooms that haven't implemented continuity of care, parents may feel the loss of a personal friendship in the strong relationship developed with the infant teacher. Your friendly interest will continue, of course, but the new staff member could be added to their group of friends, adding even more social support. If there is to be a change of caregivers, make a special effort to let the parent and the toddler caregivers get to know each other. If the transition is made gradually, time is set aside for meetings between the toddler staff and the parent, and visits to the toddler room are possible for the parent and child, their comfort level will probably increase. If you practice "continuity of care" as described on page 23, this loss will not complicate the situation.

- **Continue to personalize care.** The parent may feel that no one knows their child as intimately as the infant caregiver and no one will care for him as strongly in this new environment. Assure parents, in words and actions, that their child will continue to be respected and nurtured.

- **Take small steps.** Again, a gradual transition will help. Before the child moves, assign the new primary caregiver, if there is to be one, so that this adult/child pair can start to build their special relationship.

- **Get to know the child.** If there is a change in caregivers, allow the new primary caregiver time to observe and get to know the child while the child is still in the infant room. The caregiver should make an effort to play with the child on the floor, which is the quickest way to develop a connection with a young toddler. Let the parents see this process. Show the parents how the child's written information is also shared with the toddler staff.

- **Continue to communicate.** Parents will continue to want close communication. They enjoy and rely on the daily notes sent home that describe feeding, sleeping, diapering, and daily activities. This exact type of communication should continue as children become toddlers and two-year-olds. The toddler years will focus more on activities and cute things the child says and does during the day than on bodily functions.

- **Stay close.** Make sure that regular, "routine" mini-conferences are scheduled with parents, simply to discuss how things are going and how everyone is feeling.

Transitioning to the Toddler Room—A Child's Point of View

The key word for a successful transition from the infant room to the toddler room is *gradual*. The child is entering a new world in the toddler room. Make this new world as familiar and comfortable as possible. Again, if you practice continuity of care, almost all of the potential "trauma" or disorientation is eliminated for the child. The familiar adult is the child's anchor.

- **Arrange for the child to visit the toddler classroom frequently,** for increasing amounts of time over a period of several weeks. Start with the child's primary caregiver going along with the child and being there as the child explores in the new space, first for just a few minutes, then for longer periods of time. (Perhaps a staff swap can be arranged.) Then have the child visit without his familiar caregiver for a short time, and then increase the amount of time. Next, encourage the child to have snack with the toddlers. When he is comfortable, encourage the child to eat lunch in the toddler room, too. Finally, have the child nap with the toddlers and spend the whole day.

- **Move with friends.** The transition is easier for the child if several friends are moved at the same time. Young toddlers really do form friendships. These social bonds with other children will help the child feel less alone.

- **Remember to keep groups small.** It is still important to have small group sizes and a low child/staff ratio in toddler programs. The young toddler will be less overwhelmed with the new setting if there are only a few other children in the group.

⚜ **Plan on extra attention.** The caregivers will need to give a little extra attention to any child just entering the group. Young toddlers need close supervision. They are accident prone with their new gross motor skills and are in the climbing stage. In addition, this is the age at which children are most likely to bite each other.

TRANSITION ACTIVITY

"Moving Up" Book

Materials
camera
paper
zipper-closure bag book (see directions below)
poster board (optional)

To Make the Zipper-Closure Bag Book
Sew sandwich-size, zipper-closure plastic bags together along the bottom edge, either by hand or machine. If you cut thin cardboard such as poster board to fit inside the bags, you can use both sides. Then simply slip the pictures inside the bags on both sides of the cardboard and zip the bags shut.

To Make the "Moving Up" Book
Take photographs of the child visiting the toddler room and engaging in several of the activities, such as playing with new toys, climbing on a new climber, eating snack, playing with a new friend, and getting a hug from a new caregiver. Finally, photograph the child bringing her diaper bag to the new room and putting her "lovey" in a new cubby. Mount the photos on paper and add a few descriptive words. The last page might be a picture of the child with the sentence, "Molly is a big girl now." Place the pages in the zipper-closure bag book.

To Do
Give this book to the parents to take home and read frequently to the child, noting with pride the child's development and speaking positively about the new experiences ahead in the child's widening world.

Moving From the Toddler Room to Preschool

The same principles described previously apply when it is time to move the child from the toddlers and twos program to a classroom of older children, or a "preschool" program. This is usually, but not always, where the practice of "continuity of care" stops, and the primary caregiver starts over in the infant room. The children move up into the preschool and have a new caregiver or teacher. Generally, this transition is less traumatic because the child has language skills and is eagerly anticipating the adventures ahead.

- **Get acquainted.** Have the teachers of the preschool children visit the younger classroom to play with the children and develop a relationship with them.

- **Include parents in the decision.** Have thorough parent conferences as well and encourage the parents to observe in the older children's classroom. This decision should be based on the child's readiness, not simply because of the child's age.

- **Start with the playground.** Often there are separate playgrounds for infants and toddlers, and older children. The playground can be a great place to start visiting because the children will love the different and more challenging equipment.

- **Start well in advance.** Visits can begin a month or two before the move is made. Then, just as moving up to the toddler room, arrange longer and longer visits in the preschool classroom, especially allowing the child to use the toilet in the new setting.

- **Keep social connections.** Moving up to preschool with friends eases this transition.

- **Make a book.** A "Moving Up" book is great fun and helps the child feel that this is an accomplishment to be celebrated (see page 27).

Transitions When a Child Leaves the Program

There are many reasons that a child might leave a childcare program. The family might move, the parent's work schedule may change, or one parent may decide to stay home to care for the child. Whatever the reason, it involves loss—the breaking of a relationship. The child will suffer the loss of adult and child friendships. It can be very sad for caregivers who have cared for a child since early infancy and for other children who have formed friendships with the child.

- **Stay in touch.** Many caregivers stay in touch with families who have moved away, even attending graduations in later years. That is your personal decision, of course.

- **Make a goodbye book.** Leave the family with good parting memories. There may be photos and pieces of artwork from the child's file you can give parents at this time.

- **Have a going away party for the family.** Give other parents and the child's classmates a chance to say goodbye to the family.

- **Arrange visits.** Invite the child to come back and visit from time to time.

- **Help the parent.** Parents may be worried about finding good childcare in their new location. Provide them with information about what to look for when shopping for childcare, and tell them about local Child Care Resource and Referral agencies designed to help parents locate quality care.

Staff Transitions

Daily Transitions

In a childcare setting, children are likely to see several different caregivers during the day. Typical caregiver shifts of eight hours or less each day rarely coincide exactly with the time the child is at the center. Also, there will be "floater" staff or someone who covers the classroom while the regular caregivers take their breaks. In addition, every program will have substitutes from time to time. Do your best to limit the number of people who interact with infants and toddlers.

- **Consistency helps.** If everybody comes and goes at the same time every day, it helps the child know what to expect. *"Miss Suzie always goes home after we have our snack. Mr. Dan comes in and plays with us for a while every morning when Miss Suzie leaves the room."* When the child gets used to this, it is no longer a big issue.

- **Greet children.** When the caregivers arrive in the morning and some children are already there, or when they return from a break, they should greet each child. A greeting ritual, such as those described on page 37, might be used.

- **Say goodbye.** Just as we tell parents not to sneak out on the children in the morning, the caregivers should also tell the children that they are leaving and give them a cheerful hug goodbye, even if there are a few tears. It is much better than just disappearing.

- **Overlap.** It's nice if staff can overlap their shifts for a short time to give them a chance to share information and to make the transition less abrupt for the children.

- **Become familiar with parents.** It can be disconcerting to parents when they come to pick up their child and find an unfamiliar caregiver in the classroom. When parents enroll their child into the program they should be introduced to all of the staff who will be interacting with their child so that they may get acquainted. This can be done during the parent intake interview, parent visits to the program before the child begins attending, conferences, and special social events for families and staff. If new caregivers are in the classroom when the parent arrives, they should introduce themselves, or ask another staff member to make the introduction.

- **Be consistent in routines.** All staff, including substitutes, should be trained in exactly how things are done—feeding, diapering, toileting, hand washing, tucking in, and so on, so that the child is comfortable with the new person.

Staff Changes

A change in staff will always come as a shock to the very young child. Because infants and toddlers "bond" with their primary caregivers, the loss is more intense than when it occurs with older children. For this reason, programs are urged to do everything possible to minimize staff turnover in the infant and toddler programs, at least urging caregivers to plan ahead and leave at times when children make the transition to older groups.

- **Inform parents ahead of time, if possible.** If the caregiver is leaving on good terms and the departure is known well ahead of time, inform parents of the reason. They should not come in and be surprised by a new caregiver. They should be able to say their goodbyes and express their appreciation to the caregiver who is leaving.

- **Promote from within.** When you can, fill the position with someone known to the parents and the children to minimize the trauma associated with the change.

- **Involve parents in hiring.** When parents are involved in interviewing the candidates to fill the vacated position, they feel more responsible for making the person feel welcome. It gives the parent the knowledge that their opinion is valued, and may make them aware of the importance you place on the position.

- **Arrange for parents to become well acquainted with the new caregiver.** Post or publish a photo and biography of the new person in your newsletter. You might host an informal reception for parents to meet the new caregiver.

- **Overlap starting/leaving dates with the current and new caregivers.** It is ideal if the new caregiver can work side by side with the caregiver who is leaving. This allows the children and the parents to become comfortable with him or her, and helps to ensure consistency in the way things are done.

- **Keep things simple.** Simplify activities for the first week or two so that the caregiver can focus on getting to know the children rather than making elaborate activity preparations.

- **Allow time.** Children may be fussy or temperamental the first few days with a new caregiver. Ensure that the new caregiver has plenty of time for the everyday routines of diapering, dressing, feeding, and so on, so that no one feels pressured or rushed.

Weekend-to-Monday Transition

Any time there is a break in the routine, infants and toddlers can become temperamental. As simple a thing as coming back to the childcare center on Mondays after a busy weekend at home can be a challenge for this age group. Shopping, visiting, napping at different times, staying up late, eating on a different schedule, and so on, can throw children "off kilter." Of course, that's life!

- **Give a warm welcome.** Bring out your special welcome rituals to help children know they are back to the predictable (see page 37).

- **Communicate with parents.** Ask parents about their weekend activities. They may share things that will explain the child's behavior.

- **Keep it simple.** Go right back to your consistent routine and ways of doing things. Strive for easy, calming activities on Monday mornings. Sensory play is a good choice.

- **Look forward with optimism.** You have a great week ahead with lots of fun opportunities for children's growth and development. Communicate this with parents.

SIMPLE TRANSITIONS FOR INFANTS AND TODDLERS

Daily Transitions With Infants

Caregivers who work with infants in childcare centers sometimes feel that they are so busy with the routines of the day, feeding, and diapering children, that they don't have time for learning activities. What many fail to realize, at least at first, is that much of the "learning" children benefit from happens in the context of these basic daily routines. The most important thing to remember is to enjoy each moment. No moment of the day is more important than any other. In each interaction with you, the child is learning more about being human. Your influence is tremendous when you work with infants.

Individualize Schedules

For many good reasons, infants should be on a "demand" schedule. In other words, they eat when they are hungry, sleep when they are tired, and play and explore when they are relaxed and alert. Because of their different levels of development and their individual temperaments, children will do these things at different times. In a good infant program, it is rare to find every child doing the same thing at the same time. To manage this type of individualization well, the caregiver must be familiar with each child and able to read the signals the child puts out to

indicate what she needs. One child may tug at her ear and twirl her hair when she is tired. Another may cry and be irritable. The caregiver will learn the difference between a "hungry" cry, a "tired" cry, a "frustrated" cry, and a cry of pain for each child. Some children are very consistent from day to day and have well-established patterns of eating, sleeping, and playing. Others are more unpredictable. Being able to respond appropriately to infants is one reason for small child/adult ratios in infant programs (see section on primary caregivers on pages 22-23).

Find out as much as possible about the child to predict what his routine will be. No one knows an infant as well as the parents. Use them as the primary experts on the child. In your intake interview with parents, be sure to talk to them about their child's routines and any special tricks or techniques for holding their child's attention during mealtimes, settling her down to nap, comforting her when she is upset, and so on.

Post a written schedule for each child, so that the primary caregiver or any substitute can anticipate what to expect from the child. However, be sure to remain flexible and base your actions on the signals that the child is giving you. To do this well, you'll need to be well organized and have a sense of teamwork with other staff. Someone may need to step in and get a child who has awakened from a nap out of her crib, for instance, when you are busy feeding a baby who slept longer than expected. This flexibility and teamwork is essential with infant room staff.

It is very important to have a system for written communication with parents. Parents like to know the details of what their child does every day. Most parents read with great interest notes about what their child ate and when, diaper changes, sleep times, and play activities. However, do not allow written notes to replace face-to-face communication with parents. Be sure to tell them about the cute things their child did during the day and communicate in many ways that you enjoy taking care of their child.

SIMPLE TRANSITIONS FOR INFANTS AND TODDLERS

Morning Separation From Parent

Read Chapter 2, Center Transitions, for a discussion about introducing an infant to childcare. The advance preparation you do for this major transition has an enormous influence on the feelings of well-being of both the infant and the parents. Preparation will greatly influence how this first transition of the day succeeds on an on-going basis with infants and their parents.

Learning to part from and reunite with loved ones is a major life lesson. It can be hard for anyone, regardless of age. Parting from a parent can be difficult for very young children, especially once they reach an age of greater awareness (around seven or eight months). Their grief is often apparent. Because they have no sense of time, they may feel as though they are losing the parent forever. Do not make light of this feeling. Instead, acknowledge it, while remaining calm and reassuring.

The length of time it takes a child to adjust depends on many things. The child's temperament has a lot to do with it. Some children are very relaxed and open and accept change readily. Others are more wary and fearful. It can also depend on the child's age. Generally, younger infants adjust more quickly than those approaching toddlerhood. It also

depends on how quickly the transition has been made. Children (and parents) who have been given the great advantage of many pre-enrollment visits and gradual enrollment into childcare (see page 19) usually have a much smoother adjustment than children who are rushed into care and are just dropped off one morning.

Often, younger infants have very little difficulty separating from parents (sometimes to the parents' dismay). This is just the way the world works for them. However, especially once the child develops "object permanence" toward the end of the first year, stranger anxiety may emerge. This can be a very difficult time to enter childcare. Also, some children who were separating smoothly from their parents for several months may start to protest at this stage. They are becoming aware of the absence of the parent. In all cases, your calm, assuring manner, empathy, and acceptance of all of the emotions (rather than glossing over them or denying them) helps during this phase of life.

In this daily transition from home to childcare, parents might be experiencing the greatest distress. Some of the suggestions here will focus on the needs of parents. Remember, the happier and more relaxed the parent is, the happier and more relaxed the child will be. It is the caregiver's job to help make this transition go well for both the parents and the children.

One of the hardest things to do in life is to leave your baby with someone else, especially a "stranger." Parents will differ in their responses. Some will seem just fine, and others will literally fall apart. Caregivers must know that it is difficult for everyone. Parents need to gain trust in you as their child's caregiver and know that you will never take their place in the affections of their baby (the greatest fear of many). Talk to the parents about this in the intake interview and repeat it from time to time. Help them believe that they will always be Number One with their child, but that it is healthy for their child to develop a secondary attachment to a caregiver.

Develop Consistency

Help parents feel that they "know the ropes" in the childcare center. Parents like to know exactly where they are supposed to go and what is expected of them.

- **Have a familiar greeter.** It is very important that the same person be there to greet the parent and child each morning.

- **Notify parents of changes.** If at all possible, let the parents know the day before if there is to be a substitute or some other change. It is very disconcerting for parents to see an unfamiliar face in the morning when they drop off their baby.

- **Have a special place for the child's things.** Establish a labeled cubby or place to hang their diaper bag, and labeled bins for diapers, food, and so on. Parents should know where they should put things when they are in a hurry in the morning.

- **Make them comfortable.** It's nice to have a comfortable place for the parents to sit down while they take outer clothing off of children, and get them ready for the day. Parents should always feel comfortable in the childcare environment.

- **Welcome "security items" from home.** A teddy bear, blanket, or piece of a parent's clothing can be of great help in making the child feel comfortable in any new setting.

Welcome Ritual

To Do

Develop a little poem that involves the child's name to say in greeting when the child and parent arrive in the morning. Perhaps add a little movement with it. For instance, after you receive the child from the parent, do a little waltz as you sing the following song (to the tune of "Down by the Station"). You can vary this for each child, adjusting what you do to suit the child's temperament.

> *How are you this morning, this morning, this morning,*
> *How are you this morning, my friend, <u>Molly Jean</u>?*

The purpose of this little ritual is to give the child a solid start for the day. When exactly the same thing happens each morning when she first sees you, the child is touched and firmly acknowledged. The parent is confident that you know the child is there and that you are happy to see her. As a caution, this activity should not feel artificial or contrived, so be light and flexible and do this activity when it feels like a natural thing to do.

As part of the welcome ritual, also greet the parent by name and share a warm smile. Ask the parent about the child's night and early morning, and try to gather any other pertinent information.

Bye-Bye Ritual

To Do

Encourage parents to develop a ritual for parting with their child at drop-off time. Explain to parents that doing the same things in the same way when they say goodbye each morning helps the child, even if the child still cries. The parent should use words, actions, and gestures. Because gestures, facial expressions, and body language are more important to a very young child's understanding than words, this ritual says to the child, "*I am leaving now. We will be apart. But I love you and you love me, and I will come back.*" Each parent should come up with his or her own ritual, which can change as the child grows older.

Example

The parent says, "*Bye-bye, my sweet little one. I have to go to work now. I'm leaving you here so Miss Suzie can take good care of you. I'll be back later.*" The parent kisses the child on each cheek and then they rub noses. When the parent leaves, the caregiver can walk over to the window with the child and wave goodbye to the parent together.

Sing to a Grieving Baby

To Do

Once the parent leaves, the baby needs a caregiver to fill the void for her. Some babies may cry loudly. Others, especially younger ones, may just seem a little "blank." One of the best things you can do is to sing to the child. Hold the child against your chest and walk around or rock a bit. The vibrations of your voice and gentle hold will be deeply comforting to the child. Do this as long as the child seems to need it. Then you can put the child down and stay near, or diaper or feed the child. Stay close at first until the child seems to focus outward and wants to venture into the room.

Comfort Song

To Do

While cuddling the child, sing the following song to the tune of "Here We Go 'Round the Mulberry Bush."

> *It's hard, it's hard, to say goodbye*
> *When (Mommy) goes away.*
> *But I will take good care of you*
> *And we'll have fun today.*

Family Photo Board

Materials

bulletin board near door of room
photo of each parent and child

To Do

Ask each family to bring in a family photo, or better yet, take a photo of the smiling parents holding their child. Place these photos on the bulletin board and label them. Bring the child over to the photo when she seems to be sad and missing her parents. Talk about the photo. "*Here's a picture of Molly and Mommy. Mommy loves Molly very much.*" The baby may reach out and pat the picture. You can also point to and name the other children and their parents.

An added bonus is that this gives all the parents the opportunity to know the names of the other parents and match up which parent goes with which baby. You are creating a sense of community.

What to Do When a Parent Can't Leave

From time to time, you will encounter a parent who cannot tear herself away and leave. Sometimes the parent does not like to leave when the child is upset. On the other hand, sometimes the parent won't leave *until* the child is crying. For example, the child is playing comfortably and the mother keeps saying, *"I'm leaving now and I won't be back for a long time,"* until the child looks up and cries. What she may be doing subconsciously is proving to herself that the child loves her and will miss her. This can seem silly or frustrating to you, but keep your perspective. You are dealing with a grieving individual, someone who needs your empathy and support.

- 🥄 **Offer empathy.** Put your arm around the mother and say, *"It's really hard to leave your baby in the morning, isn't it? I know you spent a lot of time choosing where to leave her, and I promise we will take very good care of her. But, I know…it's still hard."*

- 🥄 **Invite the parent to stay and play if time allows.** If the parent must get to work, you might suggest that he or she carve out some time in the afternoon to come in and play and relax with the baby.

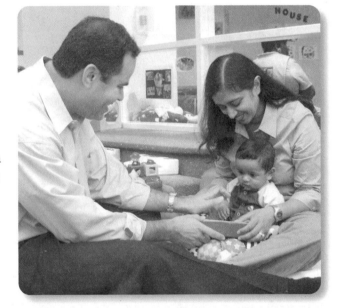

- 🥄 **Encourage the parent to develop a "Bye-Bye Ritual"** (see page 37). This can help both the parent and the child move on to the next part of their daily routine.

- 🥄 **Always say goodbye.** Sometimes the parent is tempted to tiptoe out of the room when the child is distracted or seems to be playing comfortably. Encourage parents to always say goodbye to the child, even if it causes tears. This is respectful of the child. If the parent sneaks out, the child will take much longer to learn to trust the new situation.

Transitions Throughout the Day

The transitions involved with feeding, diapering, napping, and playing fill up the day of an infant in childcare. The child is learning at every waking moment, interpreting the environment, and practicing new skills such as reaching toward objects; pointing, grasping, and releasing objects; learning to move toward objects or people; and jabbering. If the child feels some control in making things happen, it can be very pleasant for everyone involved.

Everyone likes to be informed in advance of any change, even babies. Whenever you are going to do anything with the child, such as pick her up, feed her, or diaper her, hold your arms out toward her and tell her what is going to happen. *"I'm going to pick you up now."* This way of doing things gives the child a feeling of participation, rather than just being passive. It's amazing—even very young babies will respond to you. You can see them stiffen their bodies and lean their heads forward, in preparation for being picked up. Eventually, the child will respond by holding out her arms to you, truly participating in the venture.

Mealtime

While mealtime should be relaxed and enjoyable, the transitions around feeding are sometimes tension filled, just the opposite of what you want to achieve. Often, the problem is that infants get hungry at similar times, yet they must be fed individually.

- **Try to get children on varied schedules** so that their hunger peaks at different times.

- **Have everything ready.** Try not to leave a child in a high chair or sitting in a chair at a table with nothing to do.

- **Develop teamwork.** Hold infants when they are drinking from a bottle. As much as possible, this should be a time when the infant has your full attention. If possible, work it out with other staff in the room so that you do not need to interrupt the child's feeding.

- **Supplement staff.** This is often a time when programs supplement their staffing with "floaters" or administrative staff who can come into the room for a short time and supervise the children who are not eating.

- **Feed two children at once.** When children are eating finger foods or baby foods, place two feeding chairs near each other. Both children can eat at the same time, allowing each to take her time and enjoy the experience and the interactions with you and the other child.

When Other Children Cry or Demand Your Attention

Usually in infant care, babies are bottle-fed with the caregiver holding the baby. The caregiver sits in a chair stationed in or near the play area while other children are either sleeping or playing. It is common for mobile infants to crawl over and demand your attention when you are feeding another child. You can acknowledge her, pat her head, and so on, but try not to divert your attention to the extent that your focus is on the interrupter rather than the child you are feeding.

Have you ever tried to catch the eye of a waitress in a restaurant, and although she knows you are there, she will not look at you or come over? You know the building frustration you feel in this situation. If the waitress made eye contact with you and said, "I'll be with you in a minute," you would feel less tense and it would be easier for you to wait. This is what happens when you talk to waiting babies. They may not like it, and they may not stop crying or protesting (but they might!). In any case, they will feel heard and respected. Be sure to have something for the other children to do while they are waiting.

- **Talk to the waiting children** and tell them you will be with them soon. Remember that even young children understand tone of voice. Make eye contact with the waiting child and say, *"Yes, I know, Max, you are hungry too. I am feeding Dylan right now, but as soon as I finish with him I will come and get you and feed you."* Even if they do not understand your words, they will understand your intent.

Transition to Self-Feeding

There comes a time in the infant year, not long after the child has mastered grasping and releasing objects, that the child prefers to hold her own bottle. This is also when the child will grasp at the spoon as you try to feed her. Learning to get a spoon to the mouth without turning it over takes some major practice, so be prepared for a mess.

- **Allow the child as much independence as possible.** You can still hold her while she holds her own bottle.

- **Give the child her own spoon to hold** while you continue to feed her with another spoon.

- **Let the child try to feed herself** with the spoon as long as her interest lasts. Then you can step in and feed her the rest of her meal.

Sitting at a Table

Once children can sit up unsupported, they can sit at a low table. Make sure the table is very low, not much higher than the child's waist when seated. And use low chairs that allow the children to rest their feet on the floor. Station yourself at the table and act as "social director," handing out napkins and food. Stay with them and talk about what they are eating. Allow the children to leave the table when they wish, but do not allow them to take food with them. They will learn that eating snack happens only at the table. This is an ideal way to serve snack or a simple lunch as children approach toddlerhood.

TRANSITION ACTIVITY

Come to the Table Song

To Do

Sing this to any melody that fits, such as "For He's a Jolly Good Fellow."

> *Come to the table,*
> *Come to the table,*
> *Come to the table,*
> *So you can have a snack.*

If you sing this same song every day, the children will associate it with what they are supposed to do.

Diapering

Frequent diaper checks are routine as the day progresses. It is polite to tell the children that you are going to do this. Caregivers can say, *"I'm going to see if your diaper is dry,"* before diving right in. When a child's diaper does need to be changed, hold your hands out, and tell the child you are going to pick her up and change her diaper.

- 🖐 **Use the same place.** Change the child's diaper in the same spot, your designated changing area, every time.

- 🖐 **Be prepared**. Have the needed supplies handy ahead of time. *Never leave a child unattended on a changing table at any time, for any reason.*

- 🖐 **Don't rush.** Regard diapering time as relaxed one-on-one time with a baby. You can use this time to make eye contact and sing a little song, or simply talk to the baby, imitating the baby's sounds as well.

- 🖐 **Back again.** When you are finished with everything, put the child back where she was when you picked her up unless you are going to transition the children into another activity.

TRANSITION ACTIVITY

Washing Hands Ritual

To Do

After changing the diaper, wash your hands and the child's hands. This can be a little ritual you share. Holding your hands under running water, you can sing (to the tune of "Here We Go 'Round the Mulberry Bush"):

> *This is the way we wash our hands,*
> *And rub our hands, and scrub our hands.*
> *This is the way we wash our hands.*
> *Now they're nice and clean.*
> *All done!*

TRANSITION ACTIVITY

Hand Massage

Materials
hand lotion

To Do
After the child has clean hands, use the lotion to give the baby a gentle hand and arm massage. This loving activity feels good at any time of day!

Playtime

In an infant room, the "play area" is the place where children interact when they are not involved in the routines of diapering, feeding, and sleeping. In many centers, relatively little thought is given to playtime. It's true that much of the infant "curriculum" happens during the routines of feeding and diapering. But the play area and playtime are important too! What are the transitions involved in this often neglected segment of the day? What is your role here?

Preparation

The most important part of your role at playtime happens before the child arrives, when you decide what toys and materials to make available. You know all of the children well; you know their interests and the skills they are working on. Be sure that the environment contains toys and equipment that will allow the child to practice her emerging skills. Children will be drawn to just the right toy or activity that challenges their emerging skills, so include several things to match different interests. Children will use basic toys in many different ways and at different levels of complexity, so many toys can be appropriate for younger as well as older infants.

- **Provide easy and consistent access to toys.** Keep favorite toys in the same spot, on a low shelf, for instance, so that the child can look for them and find them herself.

- **Use clear containers.** Use clear, plastic containers to store toys with many pieces so the children can see what is inside.

- **Don't overstimulate.** Try to strike a balance between having enough toys to attract and keep the child's interest and putting out too many, making it impossible for the child to make a choice and settle down.

- For specific advice on setting up the environment, see Appendix pages 148-156.

From Not Playing to Playing: Entering the Play Area

You have finished feeding and diapering the child. Now it is time to get the child settled in the play area. The best situation for most infants is to be able to move on a clean floor or blanket placed over the carpet. When children are free to focus on objects, use their muscles, and move, they are actively learning about their bodies and about the properties of objects.

- **Give a starting point.** If you have a nice, large play area, it's a good practice to put the child down in the same spot each time. This gives the child the same "starting point." This is one more act of consistency that leads children to a feeling of security and independence.

- **Be a delivery service.** If the baby is not yet moving from place to place, "scootching," crawling, or cruising around the room, you need to bring appropriate play objects over to the baby and put them within the baby's reach.

- **Place young, non-mobile babies near each other,** side by side on a blanket on the floor so they can see and enjoy being near each other.

- **Let the children move freely.** Allow the child to move toward what interests him or her.

- **Model.** From time to time, if you want to encourage the child to try a certain toy or activity, you can sit down and play with it yourself. This can greatly increase the child's interest in the toy. When the child joins you, you can either play along with the child, parallel play near the child, or back away and observe.

- **Create a social group.** Sit on the floor near a group of playing children and place the youngest infant in your lap so she can see the other children playing and enjoy the social situation.

Switching Toys and Activities

Infants switch toys and activities with very little ceremony. When a child is deeply involved in a self-chosen activity, her attention span can be amazing, which demonstrates that infants can have long attention spans. However, if they are in an exploring mood, they readily go to any interesting play object that is in their line of vision. Generally, allow the infant to set her own pace and change play whenever she wishes. She will probably make many little "transitions" within a single play period. The challenge is to make enough interesting things available to explore, but not so many that the environment is distracting or overwhelming.

From Playing Alone to Playing With Others

Infants usually engage in "solitary play," meaning that they focus on the play object rather than on other children. However, that does not mean that they are not interested in other children. Young toddlers are very interested in what other children are doing and gravitate toward the other children. With good facilitating by an adult, even infants can learn to interact and play with each other in appropriate ways.

- **Allow watching.** Infants often begin by just watching other children play. If this is their choice, let them do it. Place young children where they can easily see each other.

- **Encourage imitation.** Older infants and young toddlers like to imitate each other. Help them accomplish this by starting a clapping game, or imitating a movement you see one child doing and see if other children join you.

- **Play some simple interactive games,** such as rolling a ball back and forth, or playing peek-a-boo with several children.

The Adult's Role

It is highly advisable to have at least one caregiver in the play area any time more than one child is playing there. When you are there, what do you do?

- Stay close, and be ready to step in if it seems like one infant may hurt another.
- Help the child touch other children gently.
- Watch for hazards, for example, a child might try to pull something over on herself.
- Engage in "parallel talk," helping the child put word labels on actions and build vocabulary and providing an envelope of language.
- You could also remain quiet, observing what the child chooses on her own.
- Play with a toy to generate the child's interest in it.
- For a change of pace, interact with the children while they are playing, rolling a ball back and forth, playing peek-a-boo, and so on. However, the children should be able to choose for themselves what they wish to do.

Cleaning up

Infants are too young to clean up after themselves and to put one toy back after playing it before choosing another. Yet, sometimes children like to "help" clean up when playtime is over. Encourage this behavior as infants show an interest.

- **Lend a hand.** Involve older infants in handing you objects to put away.

- **Make it easy.** Have a well-organized environment with a labeled container or spot for each type of toy.

- 🦫 **Collect toys.** Let the children help you put all the toys in one large laundry basket. Then you place them back on the shelf.

- 🦫 **Clean up continuously.** Put things away when children have finished with them, wipe up spills, and restore order constantly throughout the day rather than waiting for a specific time to clean up.

Stopping Play

If you need to interrupt a child's play to change a diaper, feed the child, or go outside, it is usually not a problem with infants who have not yet developed the resistance for which toddlers are famous. As always, tell the child what you are going to do, and hold out your arms if you want the child to come to you or if you will pick her up. If a child is deeply concentrating on playing with an object, see if you can delay your interruption until she is finished.

As a final word about playtime, make sure that every child gets many chances to play. Too many infant programs place children in swings, walkers, infant seats, bouncers, play stations, and other devices that confine the child and prevent free movement and exploration. This shifts the child's brain into "neutral" for that amount of time when she could be actively using her brain and interacting with her world. Even young infants need to move and use their muscles. Create a safe environment and arrange for good supervision and you will not need these confining devices in the play area.

Some Developmental Transitions

Non-Mobile to Mobile Infant

An exciting developmental transition happens roughly halfway through the infant year. The child goes from staying right where you put her to moving all over the place. Infants develop many different styles of achieving this. Some children roll from one place to another. Others "scooch" along on their abdomens in an "army crawl." Often the motivation to move across space comes when the child has learned how to sit up independently. Now she can see things across the room and becomes motivated to get there.

Most babies pull themselves along on their tummies at first and gradually learn the grace and speed that comes with a raised abdomen and graduate to crawling. Some babies roll from place to place. Some babies never crawl but go directly from the "army crawl" to pulling up, to standing and cruising around while holding on to things.

- **Offer many opportunities to move freely in a safe environment.**

- **Protect the other children,** in particular those who are still non-mobile.

- **Supervise well.** Do this by staying close, ready to step in when necessary.

- **Don't "punish" the non-mobile babies** by keeping them up and out of the way in slings, swings, cribs, or other devices that don't allow them to move.

- **Divide the space.** Think of ways to section off parts of the play area with moveable bolsters or low "baby fences."

Tummy to Sitting

The best way to teach an infant to sit up independently is not to teach her. People sometimes prop babies with pillows or put them in specially designed rings to teach them to sit. The truth is that these things don't help a child learn to sit. In fact they inhibit the process. A child learns to sit by using her torso muscles, stretching, rolling, and finding her own balance. It often happens quite by accident. The child may begin on her abdomen, and then prop herself up on one elbow while using the other arm to reach for something. As she reaches, her elbow straightens out, her legs adjust themselves, and the child is propped upright, balancing herself, much to her amazement. Down she goes again! But now the child tries again and again because she is self-motivated to get into this sitting posture. Realize that she will learn to sit up only when her torso muscles are developed adequately. Propping her will not help this.

- **Let the child find her own balance**. Do nothing to help the child learn to sit.

- **Motivate with objects**. Place interesting things on the floor near the child, just out of the child's reach.

- **Acknowledge accomplishments.** Notice when the child achieves her goal. *"Wow! Look at you, Jenny. You're sitting up."*

Creeping to Crawling

Most babies begin moving by dragging themselves along with their abdomens on the floor. Eventually, they develop the technique of straightening their arms and bending their knees to get their tummies off the floor. This transition can be fun to watch. At first, the child usually is "up" for only a brief moment, almost startled at the new achievement. You will see the child experiment with this new posture over several days—up, down, up, down. Then, the child will rock back and forth on all fours. Sometimes, the child has trouble finding forward gear and when she tries to move toward an object she moves backwards instead, and may let out a cry of frustration. Finally, she figures it out, and all there is left to do is pick up speed, which some children develop to an amazing degree.

Again, there is nothing you can do to teach this, except give the child plenty of free time on the floor to learn the process herself.

Pulling Up to Standing to Walking

Allow the child the opportunity to practice. Resist the temptation to walk the child around by holding her hands, which isn't real practice. The child has to find her own balance.

- **Provide safe things to pull up on.** Have plenty of good sturdy things with which the child can pull herself up to a vertical position, such as furniture, large plastic or wooden cubes, or bars attached to the wall.

- **Let the child go barefoot.** This gives the child a better chance to use her toes for balance and gives her more sensory input.

Going Outside

Enjoy time outside every day with the infants in your care, except in extreme weather. The change of pace and change of scenery can be good for everyone. The outside environment is more stimulating to the senses than the indoor environment, adding the sensations of nature—sun, breezes, fragrances, light and shadow, and so on. How long you stay outside can vary according to weather conditions and other demands of your program.

The transition from inside to outside can be a difficult one. There is much to do. You need to make sure all of the children are in dry diapers before you go out, and then you must help them into their outer clothing and hats. Sunscreen is advisable on bright days.

- **Teamwork among staff can make the transition to the outside much easier.** In an infant program, usually at least one child is asleep, so at least one staff person must remain inside. Have some children remain inside while one or two staff go out with others. Avoid waiting until everyone is ready and then going out all together. It is not a good idea to have infants waiting around inside in heavy outdoor clothing. Instead, one staff person can go out with two or three infants and then other children and staff can join them as they are ready.

- **Use carriers.** Very young infants can be brought outside in carriages or in infant carrier slings or backpacks.

- **Spread out a clean blanket.** Place it in the shade and allow non-mobile babies to lie on it, enjoying the patterns and movements of nature from this vantage point.

- 🐚 **Experience nature.** See if you can find natural objects that are safe for infants to explore, such as large, smooth rocks and cross-section slices of logs. **Safety Note:** Supervise closely and be sure children do not put these items in their mouths.

- 🐚 **Be prepared.** Fill a tote bag with items you are likely to need outside, such as a box of tissues, a plastic bag for disposing of used tissues, pre-moistened towelettes, small paper cups, bottled drinking water, an extra child-sized hat, and so on. Hang this tote close to your door to the outside so that you can grab it on the way out.

- 🐚 **Check the play yard and get rid of any possible hazards,** such as trash that has blown in.

- 🐚 **Plan activities ahead of time.** Decide what special play equipment you will take outside for the children.

TRANSITION ACTIVITY

Going Outside Song

Sing this song to the tune of "Here We Go 'Round the Mulberry Bush" to let the children know that they will transition to outside activities soon.

> *Now it's time to go outside, go outside, go outside.*
> *Now it's time to go outside, so we can run and play.*

You can chant this song as you gather children to go outside. While you are outside, you can change the words to suit what the children are doing, for example:

> *Max is climbing up the steps, up the steps, up the steps.*
> *Max is climbing up the steps, now he's at the top.*

Going for Rides

Many great, multiple-child strollers and wagons are available to make it easy to take children for walks around the neighborhood. Children usually love these rides and even the youngest babies can get outside this way. These are especially handy when the ground is wet. Just make sure this is not the *only*, or even the primary way you get children outside. If it is the only way they see the outside, it is like viewing nature from the back seat of a car. Children need active contact with the outside environment in which they can choose their own activities and engage in numerous different play modes.

Coming Back Inside

If you can work it out with other staff, it is easier to come back inside with a few children at a time rather than a crowd. It will give you time to remove children's outer clothing and get them settled in the play area. Then the first caregiver to come in can be available to help other staff and children a few minutes later.

Again, you can adjust your chant to ease the transition.

> *Now it's time to go inside, go inside, go inside.*
> *Now it's time to go inside, so we can* [eat our lunch] (or whatever comes next).

Wash children's hands and faces when you come back indoors.

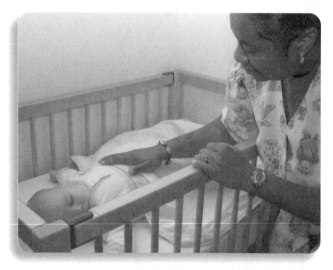

Sleeping

Young infants take two or more naps a day. Some children are regular in their sleep times, while others are quite random. During the infant year, the times and lengths of naps are likely to vary as children mature. This requires that you stay attuned to their signals of tiredness and allow children to nap when they need the rest.

Wind Down

As the child's rest time is approaching, reduce the level of physical activity and stimulation. If the child typically naps after being fed, start talking softly and perhaps sing a little "pre-lullaby" song as you change her diaper and get her ready for sleep.

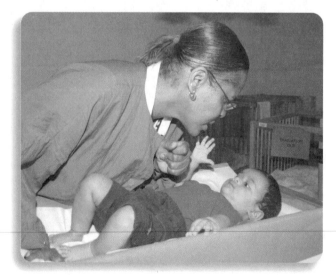

> *Soon it's time to go to sleep,*
> *All comfy in your bed,*
> *You'll snuggle in and close your eyes,*
> *And then you'll rest your head.*

Playing soft, classical music in the background is another way to calm children, as they get ready to nap.

The Transition From Wakefulness to Sleep

Some children fall asleep as soon as you put them in their cribs; others fuss, cry, or play before they slip into slumber. This is a time when sameness and consistency can really help. The child will fall asleep more easily if new things or routines do not distract her.

- **Use a primary caregiver.** It helps the child if the same caregiver puts her into her crib each day (see pages 22-23 for more information on primary caregivers).

- **Ask for advice.** Ask the parents how the child falls asleep at home.

- **Give backrubs.** You can stroke the child's head or back, while humming softly or singing a lullaby.

- **Be very boring.** This is not a time for lively facial expressions or exuberant speech.

- **Separate the space.** The sleeping area should be set aside from the rest of the environment, away from the noise and commotion.

- **Darken the room.** Dim the lights and create a soft, subdued, and relaxing feeling.

- **Create individual spaces.** Each child should have her own crib, with her name on it.

- **Be consistent.** Keep the child's crib in the same place in the room so the child sees and hears the same things each day.

- **Avoid stimulation.** It is not advisable to have toys in the child's crib, even mobiles. These are designed to occupy wakeful babies in their cribs. In childcare, children should be in their cribs only when they are asleep or falling asleep.

- **Allow security objects.** Children can benefit from having one special "lovey" stuffed animal or blanket from home as they fall asleep.

- **Serenade the child.** Sing a soft lullaby when you tuck the child in.

Lullaby

Sing this song to the tune of "Mary Had a Little Lamb."

Go to sleep, my little friend,
Little friend, little friend.
Go to sleep, my little friend,
Rest your tired eyes.

Waking Up and Transitioning to the Active Classroom

Caregivers should supervise sleep areas to be aware of when children wake up. Children should not linger in their cribs unnecessarily; when ready, they should be up and playing. Accidents can happen, and time is being wasted. A child may attempt to climb out of the crib and fall or get stuck. The child would be much better off in the play area of your classroom.

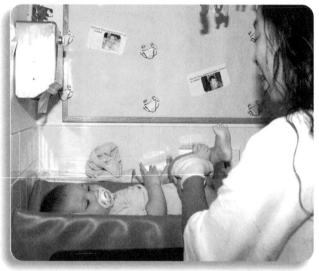

- **Let the child set his own pace.** Some children "come to" rather quickly and are ready to go, others take longer.

- **If several children awaken at the same time, you'll need to allow a few children to remain in their cribs** for the short time it takes you to change the diaper of another child.

- **Make it a soft transition into the waking world.** It can be a shock to be plunged right into the active, noisy, playing world of the rest of the room.

- **Greet the child with a warm smile.** Hold your hands out toward her, and say something like, *"I see you're awake, Maddie. I'll pick you up now so you can see your friends."* Give a hug and allow the child to "drape" on you if she needs to.

- **Try not to rush.** Infants need a diaper change immediately after waking up. Make this time relaxing and interactive.

- **Let the child join the flow of the room at her own pace.** If possible, sit down on the floor in the play area with the child on your lap and let her climb out when she feels ready.

Pretend Play Tucking In

Materials

doll bed

doll

doll blanket (a dish towel works well)

To Do

As children approach toddlerhood they begin to enjoy simple dramatic play activities. Tucking in a doll for a nap is one of the first scenarios they master. Play along and coach the child. *"Oh, look. Dolly is tired. She wants to go to sleep. Can you tuck her in? Can you sing to her?"* This type of play helps give the child a sense of mastery over a situation she has experienced many times.

Pick-Up Time

The late afternoon can be a stressful time in childcare centers. Children are sometimes tired and cranky. Parents certainly can be! The classroom may be in disarray. Unfortunately, this is exactly the time when you should look your best. To help get through this last transition of the day, create a calm atmosphere to make the end of the day pleasant and welcoming.

- **Tidy up.** As the late afternoon arrives, give your room a quick sprucing up. But don't put all the toys away behind closed doors or prohibit the children from playing. This can give the impression that your environment is sterile and boring, and, most importantly, it's not good for children either.

- **Add novelty.** Put out some toys the children haven't seen that day to interest them.

- **Lighten up.** Open the curtains or blinds and let in light.

- **Show your activities.** Add a few new instant or digital photos to the parent board that show what the children did that day.

- **Prepare the children.** Late in the day, wash children's faces and hands, put clean outfits on the children if necessary, brush hair, and prepare them to greet their parents.

- **Gather and organize materials.** Parents really appreciate it if all of their child's things are in one place, ready to go. Include in this any daily communication notes for parents, supplies needed, reminders, and so on.

- ⚜ **Offer a juice snack.** One reason children get cranky in the late afternoon may be dehydration.

- ⚜ **Create atmosphere.** Playing some soft classical music is nice.

Greet and Communicate

Have a warm smile ready and greet the parent by name. Tell the parent about the child's day. Because the late-day staff person is often not the same person parents spoke with in the morning, make sure you have any messages from the other staff available.

TRANSITION ACTIVITY

Notice the Joy

To Do

Help the parents notice the joy on their child's face when reuniting with the parent. *"Look who's happy to see you! What sparkle in those eyes!"* This is a strong way to reassure parents that you are not taking their place.

Make a collection of "happy reunion" pictures for your parent board or room scrapbook. This activity gives you the opportunity to talk to parents about parting and reuniting.

When the Child Cries at Pick-Up Time

The promotional materials of a childcare center quoted an infant teacher as saying, "I know the children love me, because sometimes they cry and don't even want to go home with their parents." You can be assured that this is not what parents want to hear! And it is not even necessarily true. The greatest fear of many parents is that their child will forget who the parent is and will love the caregiver more. You want to avoid at all costs setting yourself up in a competitive relationship with the parents.

Young infants may cry when they see their parents at the end of the day to release tension. Reassure parents that crying in this way is common for young children. You might also remind parents that this type of "reunion crying" usually happens only when the child is relatively new to a childcare program.

When the Child's Routine Changes

As babies grow and mature, their rhythms of sleep and wakefulness change. They gradually make the transition from several naps a day to just one nap. Their eating patterns change, as well as what they eat. They may go through "fussy" periods when they are teething, or when they are just about to gain a new skill such as sitting up or walking. Rather than forcing infants to comply with the routine of the room, good childcare providers make an effort to adjust their routines to meet the needs of the infant.

Communicate closely with parents about any changes in the child's routine. Share your observations between home and the center. Most centers have forms to facilitate this process, but remember the human element and communicate face to face. Your goal is to follow the child's lead. Help parents notice and take pride in their child's development.

Being an infant caregiver requires a great deal of energy and flexibility, both mental and physical. No two days will be the same for you. You need to stay on your toes and adjust your actions to the needs of the children each moment. Sometimes it may seem overwhelming. Know that your efforts make a big difference for both the children and the parents.

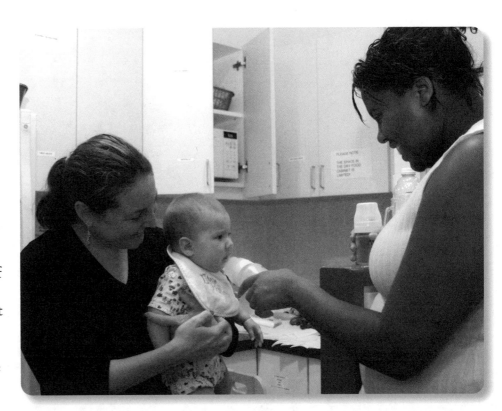

SIMPLE TRANSITIONS FOR INFANTS AND TODDLERS

Daily Transitions With Toddlers

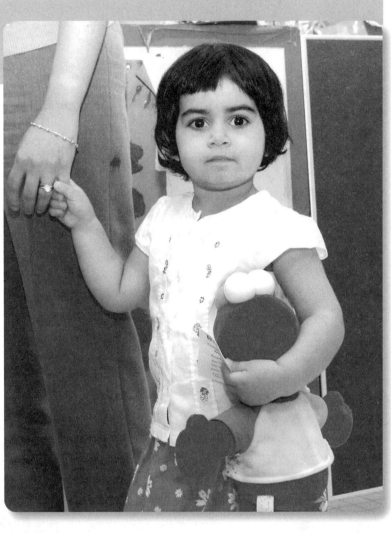

Oh, those wonderful toddlers! They practically define the meaning of "transition." They are in a transitional phase of development between being helpless, dependent babies and independent, competent preschoolers. They are evolving from nonverbal to verbal, from diaper-bound to toilet-trained, from solitary explorer to social being. The dynamics of change make children in this age group quite fascinating. See Chapter 2 pages 24-27 for more information on moving from the infant room to the toddler room.

One of the hallmarks of the toddler age is "oppositional behavior," or resisting what someone else wants. This means that daily transitions may be a little more difficult with toddlers than with older or younger children. Toddlers may feel compelled to resist you. These young human beings are testing limits and figuring out what they have control over in their never-ending quest for greater independence. And, just to make things more interesting, sometimes they are confused or overwhelmed by their power and revert back to the clingy, dependent behavior of an earlier time that felt safer.

Caregivers can do many things to make daily transitions go smoothly for toddlers. The secret lies in giving toddlers feelings of personal power and competence as they weave their way through the day. One thing in your favor is that toddlers generally like to do what everybody else is doing. Make them feel that what you want them to do is their idea, and offer many legitimate, positive choices. Create a predictable routine so they feel that they know what is going to happen next. If you work with their strong drive for independence instead of against it, you are likely to gain eager cooperation.

Morning Separation

How children act in the morning when it is time to separate from the parent varies widely from child to child. Toddlers are becoming quite social and look forward to playing with their friends. Many toddlers jump right in, eager to be part of the group. On the other hand, there are some toddlers who protest loudly; although once the parent is gone, they settle down quickly to enjoy the day. Even when the child and parent seem to be separating smoothly, pay attention to this segment of the day and reinforce toddlers' feelings of being nurtured and respected.

This is the age at which children establish their personal power. They have learned, through trial and error, how to get what they want, and they spend much effort on testing and refining their techniques. It is possible that the toddler may have given his parents several challenges before the family even arrives at school. Now he doesn't want his parent to leave. He knows that, usually, crying works. When it doesn't in this case and the parent still leaves, his cries may turn to outrage. The parent will probably feel stressed, and maybe even embarrassed at the child's behavior.

Remember, too, that toddlers are still babies. Everything written in the previous chapter about helping infants deal with separation applies to toddlers, too. This applies to their parents, as well. The parent of a toddler, especially a child who has not been in childcare before, may be going through the same feelings of loss and grief that the parent of a younger infant experiences. *"I'm losing my baby"* is a common lament of parents.

Your "intake interview"—the time you spend with the parent before the child actually starts attending on a regular basis—can be very helpful in smoothing everyone's adjustment to the new situation. The time you spend developing a rapport with the parent, a sense of ease, and a professional friendship, will pay off in easier discussions down the road. When you do a thorough job of acquainting both the parent and the child with your program with pre-enrollment visits and things to take home, such as an "All About Us" book (see page 21), a picture of you and the other children, or a toy from the classroom to borrow overnight, the child will adjust to childcare more easily, and this first transition of the day will go more smoothly from the start. (See Chapter 2 page 19 for more information on gradual enrollment.)

Talk about the child's anticipated reaction to separation. Ask the parent to predict how the child will react, and what you both will do in response.

Perhaps you could plan their "Bye-Bye Ritual" at this time. If the child reacts as you and the parents predicted, it will be easier to be gentle but decisive. The child might surprise everyone and enter the room quite easily, eager to play with the toys and the other children. On the other hand, if there is more crying than expected, you have at least discussed it with the parents and can be warm and assuring to the family.

Before the child is left with you for the first time, be sure to encourage the parent not to be tempted to sneak out when the child is looking the other way or seems to be playing contentedly. This can leave the child feeling betrayed and can even lengthen the time it takes for the child to adjust and part comfortably from the parent.

- ⚜ **Be consistent with people.** Always have the same person, preferably the child's primary caregiver (see pages 22-23), receive the child from the parent, in the same place.

- ⚜ **Have a designated place for the child's things.** A cubby with the child's name and photo on it tells the child he "belongs."

- ⚜ **Give a special greeting.** A "Welcome Ritual" such as described on page 37 is always a good idea. Be sure to use the child's name. Toddlers like the "Give me five" hand-slap routine.

- ⚜ **Encourage a ceremonious parting.** A "Bye-Bye ritual" such as described on page 37 will help both the child and the parent say goodbye.

- ⚜ **Offer a consistent first activity.** Try to do a specific activity with the child each day as soon as the parent leaves, such as feeding the fish, playing at the sensory table, or having a small snack.

- ⚜ **Allow feelings.** Rather than glossing over the child's feelings, acknowledge them and don't rush the child to get over them. Be empathetic and say, *"I know it's hard to say goodbye to Daddy in the morning. But I'm here to take good care of you, and when you're ready we have lots of fun things to do."* Remember that even if the child doesn't

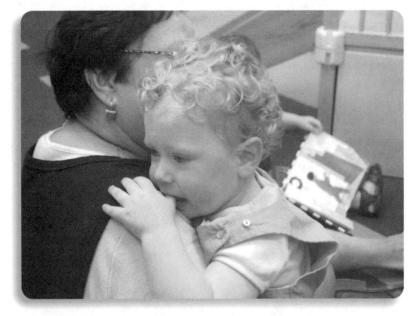

understand every word, your facial expression and reassuring tone of voice will communicate the idea to him.

🖐 **Encourage peer greetings.** Teach the other children to greet those who arrive. *"Oh, look, here's our friend, Max. Hi, Max!"*

🖐 **Offer a favorite toy.** During a pre-enrollment visit, if the child shows an interest in a particular toy, make sure to have it available on his first day.

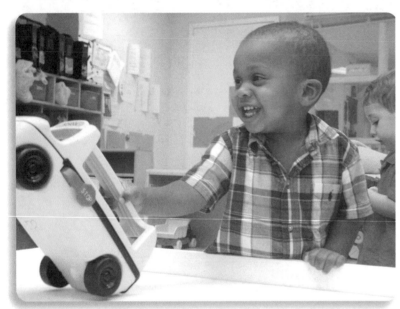

🖐 **Use toddlers' interest in having friends.** In adjustment times, point out his "friend" across the room and help him join the other child. You can describe what the other child is doing. *"Molly is trying on the new hats. Maybe you want to do that too."* But let the child decide when to scramble off of your lap.

🖐 **Offer attractive, consistent activity choices**. Even after children are well adjusted to parting from parents, set out simple but enticing activities each morning before the children arrive. Have similar choices of activities set out from day to day, such as sensory materials, blocks, and dress-up. Then add variety within those general categories to maintain children's interest. For example, offer heated playdough one day; on the next day, put out playdough with rubber stamps to press into it; on the third day, offer small wooden hammers to use with the playdough.

A Book About Us

Materials
digital (or regular) camera
printer
report binder

To Make
If you have a digital camera it is simple to create a book, keep it in an electronic file, and have it ready to print out for new children. Take a picture of the children engaging in all the activities that happen in a typical day, such as saying goodbye in the morning, playing at the sensory table, having snack, listening to a story, meeting a puppet, going outside, swinging, eating lunch, napping, playing with rhythm instruments, painting, climbing outside, another snack, and finally, greeting the parent at the end of the day. Add words to the pictures, writing it in a "Once upon a time" format, like a storybook.

To Do
Print the pages and place them in a report binder. Give it to parents to take home and read to their child.

Variation
Personalize the book by photographing the new child engaged in all of these daily activities. Be sure to include the child playing with his new friends. All children like to see themselves as the "star" of a book. This will give the child a feeling of pride and accomplishment and help him look forward to the next day.

Photos to Go

Materials
digital (or regular) camera
printer
laminating material
self-stick magnet strips

To Make
Just as you post photos of families in the classroom, it is also helpful for children to see photos of themselves at school while they are at home. Create a picture of you and the child together to post on the family's refrigerator. Take a nice, smiling close-up photo of the two of you doing something together that the child enjoys, such as playing with playdough or reading a book. This helps to build a bridge between home and the center.

Choose a Book for Later

Materials
selection of special picture books
attractive basket

To Do
Fill an attractive basket with a collection of special picture books, ones that are not part of your regular classroom collection. When the child and parent arrive in the morning, they choose a book to read together at the end of the day and put it in the child's cubby for safekeeping. At pick-up time, before rushing away, the parent and the child settle down in a cozy corner and enjoy their special book together. Then they return it to the basket. This ritual does two things: It tells the child that Daddy is definitely coming back because he agreed to read this book with him; and it gives him a very pleasant association with books, inclining him to be someone who reads for enjoyment later in life.

Empathetic Friends

To Do
When a new child is sad or cries at the departure of the parent in the morning, the other children will be naturally empathetic and may come over and just stare at him, making him even more uncomfortable. Teach the children how to respond in a friendly way. *"Max is feeling sad because he misses his mommy. What do you think will make him feel better?"* The other children are likely to come over and pat Max, bring him a tissue, give him a hug, or even bring him their special blankie. You can then say things such as, *"That was a friendly thing to do." "That made Max feel better." "See, Max? You have friends here who care about you."* These are important social lessons that will last a lifetime.

I'm Taking Care of You Song

Sing this song to the tune of "On Top of Old Smokey."

> *Good morning, dear Max*
> *I'm here to say*
> *I'm ready to take care of you*
> *Another day.*
>
> *There are lots of fun things*
> *With which you can play*
> *With all of your friends*
> *At [your center's name] today.*

Pretend Phone Calls

Materials

2 toy telephones or cell phones that are no longer in use

To Do

Once children develop some simple language skills you can use this activity to help comfort them when they are missing their parents. Suggest that the child pretend to call a parent at work. You take on the role of the parent. Together you can have a conversation that might go something like this:

> Together: *Make the sound of ringing phones.*
> You: *"Hello, this is Mommy. Who is this?"*
> Child: *"Me!"*
> You: *"Oh, is this my dear little Max? I hope you are having lots of fun today. I can't wait to see you!"*
> Child: *"I love you, Mommy."*
> You: *"I love you too, Max. I'll give you a big hug when I come to get you this afternoon. Till then, have fun playing!"*
> Child: *"Bye!"*
> You: *"Bye!"*

You might have to coach the child on the lines (then again, you might be surprised!).

Family Photos

Children find comfort in having pictures of their family with them during the day. If parents don't have family pictures they can leave with you, perhaps you could take photos when parents come to drop off and pick up their children. Take advantage of moments when children look at these pictures to talk about their families. There are many ways you can make these photos accessible to children, such as:

- Make a photo album with a section for each child in your group. Place this in your reading nook where children can look at it at any time.
- Make a separate little photo book for each child's family pictures, perhaps using zipper-closure bag books (see page 27).
- Laminate photos, punch a hole in one corner of each, and place them on a large key ring for children to carry around with them.
- Place photos on a low display area where children can go up and touch them anytime.
- Make a family-matching board game. Have two copies of each photo. Laminate them. Mix them up in a box and let the children find the matching pairs.

Families Door Board

Toddlers love any kind of hinge or flap. This is really a modified form of peek-a-boo.

Materials
2 large pieces of poster board
scissors
photos of children's families
glue
tape

To Make
Cut as many "doors" as there are children in your group on the top piece of poster board. Glue the photos on the bottom board so they will show when the doors are opened. Tape the two pieces of poster board together.

To Do
Let the child "knock" on one of the doors and then open it. *"Oh look! Whose family is that? That's right, that's Max's family!"*

Love Stories and Love Songs

Materials
tape recorder
blank cassette for each child

To Do
Invite the parent to record a favorite story or sing a song or two on the tape. They could also say things such as, *"Mommy loves you so much! Here's a great big pretend hug: Put your arms around yourself and squeeze now…mmmmmmmm!"* Let the child listen to this tape when he is missing his parent.

Pretend Play About Saying Goodbye

Materials
doll or stuffed animal
briefcase (if parent uses)
lunchbox (if parent uses)
coat

To Do

Help the child act out dropping a child off at childcare. Encourage the child to play the part of the parent, and, of course, the doll plays the role of the child. You can still be the teacher. Let the child act out his "Bye-Bye Ritual" and reassure the doll that he will be back. You might have to do some of the talking for a younger child. Be sure to act out your role as the teacher by doing the same loving and reassuring things that you usually do with the child. This gives the child a feeling of power and helps to work out the emotions.

TRANSITION ACTIVITY

Homemade Book: "Mommy Comes Back"

Materials
camera
small loose-leaf binder
paper that fits in the binder
clear self-adhesive paper or laminating film
hole punch
pen

To Do

Take photos of all the steps of the child's morning routine and arrival at your program. Ask the parent to provide photos of the child's morning routine at home: waking up, getting dressed, eating breakfast, and getting into the car. Photograph the child arriving with the parent, and photograph the parent taking off the child's coat and hanging it in the cubby, hanging up the diaper bag, and hugging the child goodbye. Next, take several photos of what the child typically does during the day: playing, eating lunch, napping, and so on. Finally, photograph the end of the day: his joyous reunion with his parent; putting on his coat; and waving goodbye to his teacher and friends.

Glue these photos, in sequence, to separate pieces of paper and add a brief caption. Laminate the pages or cover with clear contact paper, use a hole punch to put holes in each page, and place the pages in the binder.

Read this homemade book to the child when he is missing his mommy or daddy. You could create a "generic" book of this type, by using pictures of all of the children. For example, include photos of Molly getting into the car, Michael arriving at school, Max putting his coat in his cubby, and so on.

All of the children, even those who separate from parents easily, can enjoy and benefit from books that deal with the topic. You can read these to children one on one, or with a small group.

Will You Come Back for Me? by Ann Tompert. Illustrated by Robin Kramer. Suki is worried about being left in childcare for the first time. Her mother reassures her that she loves her and will always return for her.

Have You Seen My Duckling? by Nancy Tafuri. One adventurous baby duckling swims away from the others. Mother and the other ducklings travel over the pond asking the inhabitants of the pond, "Have you seen my duckling?"

Where Is Baby's Mommy? by Karen Katz. The baby searches for mommy in this story with easy-to-lift flaps. A delightful interactive book.

Blueberries for Sal by Robert McCloskey. A gentle adventure story that is just right for toddlers. An excellent book for transitioning from baby books to more complex stories.

Good-Bye Daddy! by Bridgette Weinger. Illustrated by Alan Marks. A little boy must say goodbye to his father because they live in different homes. The love and caring shown by the father helps with the separation.

Hello! Good-bye! by Aliki. There are many different kinds of hellos and just as many kinds of goodbyes. Each can be filled with excitement and surprise.

Transitional Objects

A transitional object, sometimes called a security object or "lovey," can be very comforting to toddlers in childcare. Many children have already established one of these in their lives—a teddy bear or other stuffed animal, a blanket, Dad's old hat, and so on—that they like to take to bed with them and generally haul around during the day. If the child doesn't have one, you might suggest that the parent select something that could

be used for this. When children see the other children with their "loveys" at nap time, they may want one, too. It's amazing to see the strength the child can pull from his special object. There's magic in that stuffing material! Holding on to a teddy bear can give the child the courage to face the world. This is the child's first use of a symbol. The object symbolizes home and comfort.

At first the child may want to have his security item with him all the time, and admittedly, it can take some managing from toddler teachers. Try to stay flexible. Eventually, the child will find it cumbersome and you'll be able to convince him to leave it in his cubby, saying he can go and get it when he needs it. The item then comes out only when the child is not feeling well or is hurt, and always during rest time.

Children are very possessive about their security items. Usually other children understand that this is the child's special "lovey" ("...*just like your blanket, Molly*") and he doesn't have to let other people play with it.

- **Create a duplicate.** See if you can convince the child and the parents to have one security item that gets to stay at the center and another that stays at home. This simplifies things for the parent in the morning leaving the house, and in the late afternoon at the center.

- **Have limits for security items.** For example, create a rule that states, "No 'loveys' outside or at the lunch table."

- **Keep them in cubbies.** Encourage children to keep their security items in their cubbies most of the time, bringing them out only when they are distressed or hurt, and at nap time.

Have a "Lovey" Party

Materials

security objects or "loveys"

refreshments

party hats

picture book about security objects, such as any of those listed on page 71

To Do

Ask each child to get his security object. Have a few extras for children who don't have theirs with them that day. Grown-ups should bring in their own "loveys" for this special event. You could ask each child what his "lovey's" name is, and introduce yours. Sing the "Lovey Song" below. Let children put party hats on themselves and their "loveys." Read one of the books listed on the next page. Have refreshments! (This could be your snack for that part of the day.) Let children "feed" their "loveys." Then sing "Rock-A-Bye, Baby" and have them tuck their security items back into their cubbies. Toddlers can be quite imaginative and can personify their blankies. For children who have other security objects, you could have them substitute a favorite stuffed animal. They will still enjoy the activity.

Lovey Song

Sing this song to the tune of "Me and My Teddy Bear."

You are my (child's name for object) dear,
You always wipe away my tears.
You give me comfort, you give me joy.
You're my favorite toy.

When I'm sad I bring you out.
You help me smile instead of pout.
When I go to sleep, you're in my bed.
Then I can rest my head.

I take you everywhere I go.
No matter where, this I know
When you're along, I have no fear,
I love my [child's name for object] dear.

Loveys in Literature

Materials

picture book about a security object

To Do

Invite the children to bring their special toy or security object to the story corner. Read the book to everyone. Compare their "loveys" to the object in the book and talk about how the character uses or plays with his special comfort toy.

READ BOOKS ABOUT SECURITY OBJECTS

How a Baby Grows by Nola Buck. Illustrated by Pamela Paparone. An active story about the things a growing child sees, needs, speaks, hears, and shares.

Tom and Pippo Read a Story by Helen Oxenbury. Tom exhausts his father by asking him to keep reading books to him. At last, father thinks he is finished, but clever Tom decides that Pippo, his pet monkey, also needs a story.

The Bear Went Over the Mountain by Rosemary Wells. The specific action of the bear is illustrated as he takes his trip over the mountain with his basket. His basket is empty when he starts, but full of flowers when he arrives home.

Golden Bear by Ruth Young. Illustrated by Rachel Isadora. A beautifully illustrated story about a little boy and his perfect companion.

Carl Goes to Day Care by Alexandra Day. Mom drops off the baby and Carl (her dog) at the childcare center. The teacher gets locked outside and Carl takes over. This story encourages children to use their imaginations.

Tom and Pippo by Helen Oxenbury. The first story that Helen Oxenbury wrote when she created Tom and Pippo. It's the story of a young boy and his toy monkey that goes everywhere with him. All of the **Tom and Pippo** books are full of expressions and feelings that are common to young children.

Barney Is Best by Nancy White Carlstrom. Illustrated by James Graham Hale. A trip to the hospital can be scary but it's not bad if you have a special friend along with you.

Establishing the Daily Schedule

One of the best things you can do is to establish a good, stable daily schedule of routines. Always do things in the same order. The children come to know what to expect and you will get much more automatic cooperation. Of course, you can vary what you do within those segments of routine.

Here is a sample of what a day might look like in a toddler classroom, but vary this according to the needs of your own setting. It is understood that diapering and toileting will happen on a "demand schedule," more often than listed here.

Sample Daily Schedule

7:00 – 8:30	Children arrive; several simple activity choices set out
8:30 – 8:45	Morning gathering time
8:45 – 9:00	Morning snack
9:00 – 10:00	Playtime inside
10:00 – 10:15	Cleanup time
10:15 – 10:30	Mini-circle time—puppet, story, song
10:30 – 10:45	Diapering, toileting, prepare to go outside
10:45 – 11:30	Outside time
11:30 – 12:00	Lunch
12:00 – 12:15	Prepare for nap time
12:15 – 2:15	Nap time
2:15 – 2:30	Wake up, toileting, diapering
2:30 – 2:45	Afternoon snack
2:45 – 3:20	Playtime
3:20 – 3:30	Cleanup time
3:30 – 3:45	Diapering, toileting, prepare to go outside
3:45 – 4:30	Outside time
4:30 – 4:45	Juice snack and freshen up
4:45 – 5:00	Stories, puppet, circle games
5:00 – 6:00	Simple play activities while parents come to pick up children

- **Give yourself plenty of time** for the basic routines. Start some things a little earlier, if necessary.

- **Use teamwork.** Some activities, such as diapering, putting out cots, going outside, and cleaning up can be started by one staff person while another is still involved with other children.

- **Create balance.** Alternate active times and quiet times to maintain everybody's energy and ability to concentrate.

- **Anticipate.** Talk to the children about what will happen next a few minutes before the next segment of the routine is to start.

Daily Schedule Photo Line

Materials

camera

laminating material

low wall space

To Make

Take a photo of every segment of your daily routine: arrival, morning snack, diapering and toileting, hand washing, playtime, outdoor play, and so on. Laminate these photos and arrange them horizontally, in order, on a wall at children's eye level.

To Do

Play little games to familiarize the child with the photos. See if the child can find the picture of what is going on in the classroom now. Then see if he can tell you what is happening in each photo. Bring several children over to the photos and ask them to find certain times of day on the pictures. *"Molly, can you find the picture of snack time?" "Max, which picture shows us at nap time?"*

Later, you can use this line to help children understand when things are going to happen. You can point to the picture of what will happen next and let the child tell you about it. Are you expecting a special visitor? Show children when the visitor will arrive. When a child is missing his parent, you can point to the place on the chart when the parent will arrive to pick up the child.

Morning Gathering Time

This transition activity launches the day and sets the tone. Do this at a time when all or most of the children have arrived. It gives your day a definite start.

- **Keep it short.** With young toddlers, this gathering time doesn't have to be more than five minutes or so. You can make it a little bit longer with older children.

- **Don't force participation.** If a child doesn't want to sit and listen, don't spend a lot of energy hauling him back. This only creates negative feelings about coming together. Eventually, he will participate.

- **Use the time for set-up.** While one staff person is leading the gathering time, other staff can be setting up any planned play activity and getting the room ready for playtime.

Gathering Song

Sing this song to the tune of "He's Got the Whole World in His Hands."

> *Everybody, come over here…*
> *Molly and Tiffany, come over here,*
> *Max and Toby, come over here,*
> *It's time to say hello.*

To Do

Walk around the room and take children by the hand as you sing this to bring them over to your regular gathering spot. When everyone has gathered, you can launch right into the greeting song below.

Greeting Song

Sing this song to the tune of "He's Got the Whole World in His Hands."

> *Hello, Brianna, how are you?*
> *Hello, Molly, how are you?*
> *Hello, Max, how are you,*
> *How are you this morning?*

Keep singing this, adding verses, until you have mentioned every child's name.

Puppet Takes Attendance

Materials

pet puppet
puppet's house (basket or box)

To Do

Let the children help you wake up the puppet in his house. The puppet can come out and yawn, rub his eyes, and look around. *"Look, Herkimer, everybody is here."* Puppet: *"Really, everybody? Well, I want a kiss from Molly. Now I want a kiss from……Max. Where is Toby? Oh! There he is wearing his yellow shirt. I want a kiss from Toby…"* The puppet can acknowledge and kiss each child in the group. This makes each child feel acknowledged and important.

If you have a new child in the group, you can make a formal introduction. *"Guess what, Herkimer? We have someone new here today. This is Sara."* Puppet: *"How do you do, Sara? My name is Herkimer. May I give you a kiss?"*

Who's Here Today? Cards

Materials

laminated photo of each child in the group
box with lid

To Do

Place all of the photos of the children in the box. Open the lid and take out one photo at a time. Ask the children, "*Who is this?*" ... "*That's right — it's Molly. Is Molly here today?*"

Other Possibilities

- With self-stick Velcro, attach the cards to a piece of poster board or a wall display.
- Attach self-stick magnet strips to the backs of the photos and place them on a magnetic surface.

What Will Happen Today?

Materials

photo or drawing of materials and activities you will be doing with children

To Do

Talk to the children about what you're going to do that morning. Show them pictures of the different activities. Showing them a picture of playdough, for instance, gives them a visual symbol for something they will experience—a cognitive activity. You could present four or five pictures and with each, ask a particular child what he would like to do first. This can be your way of starting children in certain play activities to begin your playtime.

Snack Time

Food is social. It gives children a chance to pause and shift gears, truly a "transitional" activity. There are two ways of presenting snack time to toddlers. The most traditional is to have everybody come and sit down at a table and eat the snack together. Another way is to have the food there and allow children to come and go as they wish. Both methods can work fine with this age group.

Traditional Snack Time

In this type of situation, everyone comes to the table at the same time and has their snack together. This is probably the easiest way to handle snack time with toddlers because of their propensity to all do the same thing at the same time. You can pick a different child each day to help you pass out the napkins and cups.

One advantage of this type of snack time is that it serves as a mini-group time, emphasizing language development. Use this time to talk with the children around the table, what they are wearing, what they did that morning, who's not there, or what they are eating. Then tell them what is going to happen next.

Come and Go Snack

In this type of snack service, place the food at the table during the playtime and the children can come and eat whenever they wish…or not. The only rule is that they stay at the table while they are eating. An adult should be stationed at the table to talk to them while they eat. This works especially well when you serve snack outside on the playground, giving you a longer, uninterrupted playtime outside.

TRANSITION ACTIVITY

Come to the Table Song (see page 42)
Sing this to any melody that fits, such as "For He's a Jolly Good Fellow." If you sing this same song every day, the children will associate it with what they are supposed to do.

> Come to the table,
> Come to the table,
> Come to the table,
> So you can have a snack.

TRANSITION ACTIVITY

Feed the Hungry Wastebasket
Children can learn to put their napkins in the wastebasket when they leave the table. It's even more fun if the container has a face on it. The wastebasket almost becomes a puppet. You could even make it talk: "Yum, yum, yum!" when children put their trash in it.

The Transition Into Playtime

Surprisingly, the transition from "not playing" to "playing" can be a tricky one for some children, and it's one we rarely think about. You have a beautiful room with many interesting play choices for children. What makes a child choose a certain activity? Often the child goes to the familiar—what he has played with before. Sometimes, the child is drawn to what other children are doing, or to a particular child. Maybe the child is attracted to a new toy, or to wherever a favorite adult has landed. Here are some tips that can help.

- **Have a clearly organized room.** Working with toddlers, you are less likely to have formal "interest centers" such as in a preschool classroom. However, you can put similar toys together and divide your space with room dividers or furniture. Your areas might be small toys and manipulatives, dramatic play, blocks and trucks, gross motor, art and sensory, and a cozy corner with books.

- **Make it easy to find things.** Store toys with many pieces in clear plastic containers so children can see what is inside.

- **Don't move things around very often.** Keep toys in the same place where the children can find them easily. This gives children a sense of security and control.

- **Have picture indicators for where things go.** Take a photo of the toy and affix it to the shelf or wall space where the toy is to be stored, as well as on the container for the toy if there is one. Cover these photos with clear contact paper. This turns clean-up time into a matching game.

- **Always have a sensory play choice.** Use water or other pourable materials in your sensory table, such as sand or confetti. Also consider using playdough or clay in the sensory table. When children have a hard time choosing an activity, this can be a good place to start. It is also good for children who are tense or upset because these materials tend to be soothing. This is a good social entry point as well, because there is usually someone at the sensory table.

- **Offer clear choices.** If you have good display of materials on shelves, children can see what they want and make a decision about where they want to play. On the other hand, if everything is all mixed up and the child merely sees a jumble of toys, the child is more likely to be overwhelmed and just dive in and start throwing things.

- **Draw attention to certain toys.** Decide to "highlight" certain toys or play activities by setting them out on a table, hanging certain dress-up clothes in a prominent place, or bringing out a piece of moveable equipment, such as a tunnel, into the middle of the play space.

- **Talk about what play choices are available.** Right before your playtime (while you are finishing snack or story time), bring out the pet puppet and ask what's going to happen next. Tell the puppet what's in store. *"Well, Herkimer, today there is water in the water table and some of the kids will be over there near the sink playing with that. And Miss Sherri will have some fun rubber stamps over where we play with playdough. Max and Molly might want to play with the dress-up clothes in the play kitchen. And, of course, the big blocks are over in the corner..."*

- **Start children in a particular place.** Be a benevolent dictator for five minutes and start each child in a certain place. Pick a few children to use the water table, and then decide where to position the other "players" in your environment. If you're a good guesser, you might be able to position children from the beginning in an activity that will draw their deep attention. Give some thought, also, to who will play near each child and the play partners you'd like to see together. But let that be the end of your dictatorship, and if there is a strong protest from a child who would rather play with something else, try to honor that. The idea of playtime is that children can choose the activity they want, because usually they choose just the right thing to practice one of their many emerging skills.

- **Expect movement.** Don't expect a toddler to stay at one thing for the whole play period, although some will surprise you and do just that. Allow them to move from one activity to another.

TRANSITION ACTIVITY

Where Does This Go?

Materials
pet puppet
various toys from the room

To Do
Bring out your pet puppet. He can tell the children that he is having a problem. He wants to put some toys away but he doesn't know where they go. He asks the children for their help. *"Max, will you show Herkimer where we put the trucks?"* This makes the child feel proud and confident and gives everyone a good review of where to find things.

Can You Find This?

Materials

photos of toys in the room

To Do

Put all the toys in their designated space. Then, show a picture of a toy to one or more children. Ask them if they know what it is. Then see if they can find it. Ask them to get it and bring it to you, but don't tell them where to find it. This provides a good review for the children.

Play Entry Skills

Some children are more skilled than others at entering into play with other children. This is another type of transition where children might need help at first. For instance, it is not uncommon for a child who lacks experience playing with others but wants to join in the play to just run into the play scene and bust everything up, causing general outrage, when all he or she really wanted was to be included. Another child may just stand back and watch the other children, longing to be part of the action, but not knowing how to join in. Ease these transitions with the following tips.

- **Have duplicate or similar toys.** Because imitation is a major play style of toddlers, simply provide toys that will make it possible.

- **Help the child notice what the other kids are doing.** Then help the child figure out what he can do alongside the other children. Most toddlers engage in parallel play. They like to do the same thing the others are doing. If they are digging in the sandbox, find another shovel and pail for the non-player to use, so that he doesn't do something incongruous, such as drive a riding toy into their midst.

- **Join in as a co-player.** Parallel play next to the child, or between the child and the group of children he wants to join. The other children will probably want to include you in their play, because an adult is a desirable playmate. Include the new child as you join the play circle, and then, gradually, as everyone gets involved, back out of the play and just observe. Eventually, let them play independently.

- **Partner the non-player with a more skillful player.** There might be one child who is "queen of the housekeeping area." A new child could be introduced to the area and the "queen" might take over, bringing dress-up clothes for the child to put on, or suggesting a role. Again, as a co-player, you can be useful in facilitating this.

⬇ **Help the children notice who wants to play.** Encourage children who are playing to see if someone is watching them and would like to play with them. *"Molly has been watching you. It looks like she wants to play with you."* This statement alone could lead to spontaneous inclusion. Usually, toddlers have not entered the "you can't play with us" stage.

⬇ **Get something fun started yourself and see who joins in.** When the play gets going, you can back away. Examples of such spontaneous play might be dancing to music, rolling a ball down a ramp, or lining up chairs to play "bus."

⬇ **Join in spontaneous toddler-invented games.** Others may join you. Again, gradually back out of the play and observe. An example: One or two children are sitting on a log on the playground. One purposely falls off backwards and puts his feet in the air. The other child copies him. You could say, *"That looks like fun. I think I'll do that too."* Other children may join in, and soon you have a fun, large group, toddler-invented game going. You are showing new players how to see what other children are doing and join in.

⬇ **Praise good play behavior.** Notice when a child successfully enters a play situation, or when other children include someone watching. *"That was a friendly thing to do." "That made Max happy."*

- 🍂 **Provide activities that are easy to participate in with other children.** When children have successful experiences in sharing a space or materials, they develop friendly relationships that make more challenging situations go a little better. Examples of easy side-by-side activities are fingerpainting on a tabletop with shaving cream, scribbling on large paper taped to a tabletop or wall, and sticking things such as yogurt container tops or laminated pictures to contact paper that has been attached to the wall, sticky side out. Bubbles and other sensory play are also "easy" activities for children to enjoy with others.

- 🍂 **Follow-the-leader games make for easy participation.** Imitation is a typical play style of toddlers, so this is a natural. Notice when one child is starting to move in an interesting way, or making an interesting noise, and start doing it yourself. Soon other children will follow.

TRANSITION ACTIVITY

Copy Me Song

Children love to sing and move to this song (sung to the tune "London Bridge Is Falling Down"). Sing it spontaneously indoors or outdoors when the children seem to need something to do together, or use it in circle time, giving each child a chance to be the star.

> *Can you do what I do, I do, I do?*
> *Can you do what I do, just like me?*
>
> *Can you jump like Molly, Molly, Molly,*
> *Can you jump like Molly, just like her?*
>
> *Can you run like Max does, Max does, Max does?*
> *Can you run like Max does, just like him?*

Toddler Friendships

As we talk about children's play skills, it is worthwhile to take a slight deviation from our focus on transitions and think about the topic of toddler friendships. If children are "friends" they are much more likely to play well together. But the topic of friendship is a new one to these inexperienced human beings. They will benefit from some coaching from you. Be assured that they are very interested in other children and want very much to have friends.

How Do Toddlers Form Friendships?

Familiarity helps toddlers build friendships. Keep your groups consistent. If children interact with the same group from day to day, they learn what to expect. Toddlers like things that are predictable and familiar. When caregivers teach children movements to a song, or have them wear hats when they go outside, they help to build this feeling of familiarity.

While toddlers vary in their ability to express themselves verbally, using words is still not the mode of communication they depend on. They cannot go up to a potential playmate and say, *"Hey, do you want to go over there and play with blocks together?"* Instead, they use nonverbal cues. They make eye contact with the other child. Sometimes they smile at the other child. They move closer to the potential friend. They imitate what the desired friend is doing. Or they do something to attract attention, such as make a wild giggle or a funny noise, or fall down and laugh. If successful, the other child will pick up on the action and join in.

How Do Friendships Affect Play?

When children are friends, the quality of their play increases. They play longer and "richer" and use a wider variety of ideas. Synergy is born! Of course, the solitary play of infants and young toddlers has its value. Children are gaining cognitive and motor skills as they play with objects by themselves. However, when they parallel play and interact with other children they gain social and creative skills along with the cognitive and motor skills of solitary play.

This is not to say that toddler friends don't fight...they certainly do. But that's not all bad. Part of being a friend is learning how to "fight" or have a conflict and work it out again. If a child has a friendship connection with another child, he will feel more deeply and will be more likely to learn the consequences of both positive and negative behaviors.

Their desire to be near each other and similar to each other leads to the familiar toddler play styles of imitation, parallel play, and herding. Imitation is their way of introducing themselves to each other. *"Hi! I'm like you. I can do that too."* Parallel play is when they do the same type of thing side by side or near each other, for instance, several children might dig in the sand together. One starts making a noise, and the others follow. "Herding" is discussed on page 100.

How Can Adults Encourage Children's Friendships?

Teach them the names of other children. It's easier to be a friend when you know what to call someone. Use their names when you talk to them and find songs and games where you can insert children's names. The photo book activities, such as "A Book About Us" (page 63) and "Who's Here Today? Cards" (see page 75) are good ways to review children's names.

Interpret children's words, facial expressions, and feelings to help children communicate with each other. *"Max, Molly wants to sit next to you." "That made Max feel good when you brought him his teddy bear. That was a friendly thing to do." "Look at Molly. She's smiling. She's happy that you gave her some of your playdough."*

Why Is It Important That Toddlers Have Friends?

Friendships enhance learning. Children get ideas from each other. Most important, with gentle adult guidance, children learn the give and take required to get along. These skills last a lifetime.

Conversely, negative social behaviors, such as bullying and hurting others, will snowball if they are not corrected early (in the toddler and early preschool years). The "rough" toddler becomes the preschooler whom other children avoid. The child starts to feel isolated and more needy and may continue to act out in ever-greater ways, beginning a cycle that can be much harder to modify in the school years. This has a negative effect on the child's self-esteem and even his ability to learn. So, modify this behavior early and teach friendship skills in the toddler years when you can really make a difference.

- **Build similarity.** Teach children simple songs, games, and rituals that they can do together.

- **Give them something similar to wear.** Two very different-looking children suddenly look like each other (to themselves, anyway) when they are both wearing fire hats. Having children wear hats when they go outside helps friendships form and protects them from the sun.

- **Keep groups together.** Move children to new classrooms in "friendship groups."

- **Encourage imitation.** Help the children figure out how they can mirror what the other child is doing.

- **Teach names.** Use children's names when you talk to them.

- **Use the words "friend" and "friendly" often.**

- **Encourage children to help each other.**

- **Plan pro-social activities.** Find as many activities as you can that are more fun to do with someone else than alone. These build successful experiences in interacting with others. Examples: rocking boat or any seesaw-type equipment made for toddlers, simple circle games such as Ring Around the Rosie, or playing with a ball.

- **Read books about friends.** Develop a collection because this is a popular topic with toddlers.

READ BOOKS ABOUT FRIENDSHIP

Listed below are picture books about friendship. Reading these to children can help them experience the give and take required in friendly relationships. Talk about this with the children, or even have them act out (with your help) parts of the books.

All Fall Down and Clap Hands by Helen Oxenbury. These are two of a four-title series of large-format board books for babies and toddlers. Helen Oxenbury's double-page watercolor illustrations are filled with big, beautiful multi-ethnic babies enjoying the active rhyming text related to the actions the babies are doing.

Tom and Pippo Make a Friend by Helen Oxenbury. Tom and Pippo find themselves playing in a sandbox while making a new friend.

Baby and Friends by Paul Bricknell. This is a title from one of the best, soft padded board-book series, with photographs of babies with their toys and their furry friends, and babies interacting together.

First Friends by Lenore Blegvad. Illustrated by Erik Blegvad. Making new friends is the theme of this delightful story. Toddlers are playing with their toys independently and as the story progresses, children begin to share their toys and play together, without the assistance of an adult.

Friends by Rachel Isadora. Children are busy playing, jumping, and drawing in small groups and alone. These familiar scenes delight children as they listen to the story.

Friends at School by Rochelle Bunett. Photographs by Matt Brown. These full-color photographs tell the story of children with a variety of abilities playing together. This book shares the importance of inclusion for all children.

Moonbeam's Friend by Frank Asch. This board book is a simple story of friendship between Moonbeam (a big bear) and bird, his very small friend.

At Preschool With Teddy Bear by Jacqueline McQuade. Teddy Bear is ready for his first day at preschool and at the end of the day he can hardly wait to get home to share his day with his cat.

TRANSITION ACTIVITY

Homemade Book About Friendliness

Materials
small photo album or zipper-closure bag book (see page 27)
camera or drawing materials

To Make
Think of a very simple friendship gesture you might witness the children share and create several pages that depict the exchange. For instance: Page 1: Molly fell down and hurt her knee. Page 2: Max saw Molly cry. He wanted to help her feel better. Page 3: Miss Suzie washed Molly's knee and put a Band-Aid on it. Page 4: Max brought Molly her bunny. Page 5: Molly feels better. Either use photos (you might even get the children to pose for them) or draw simple pictures.

To Do
Read this book to the children and then talk about friendly things to do.

Moving From One Play Activity to Another

Adults, rather than children, usually have a problem with moving from one play activity to another. The key to not becoming frustrated is to have appropriate expectations. While children occasionally will amaze us with their attention spans, it is more typical for children to spend a short time playing with something and then move on to something else. This is partly because of their distractibility. Don't expect them to finish what they start, and don't expect them to remember to put one thing away before they start something new. As a caregiver, you can be there to coach and help, or you might decide that it is more valuable not to interrupt their play, and simply put the toy away yourself. It is not necessarily a bad thing for toddlers to go from one activity to another. They are explorers. They should feel that they have free rein of the environment and can make their own choices, even spontaneous ones.

- **Join in.** Play with the child yourself as he engages with the toy. This dramatically increases a child's perseverance with a toy.

- **Don't overwhelm.** Put out a more limited assortment of toys so he won't be so distracted.

- **Cut down on visual distractions.** Put up low room dividers to create many nooks and crannies in your environment where children play.

Sharing and Taking Turns

This is the transition between having something and not having it; or having it alone and having it with someone else. Can sharing and taking turns be regarded as "transitions?" They can, because they mark the transition between playing alone and playing with others, from being a loner to being a successful social being. In any case, it is important learning. It is not true that toddlers cannot share or take turns. But these are very new skills that they are just learning. They will need a lot of support from you. You need promote many successful experiences in sharing and taking turns. Then talk about how they are sharing the materials or taking turns, so they are conscious of doing it successfully. When these guided activities are experienced repeatedly, the children will be more successful in coming up with strategies spontaneously while playing with other children.

- **Have an interesting activity for the waiting child to do.** Waiting will be much easier if the child waiting is engaged in something interesting such as kicking a new ball or playing with the teacher, rather than just gazing longingly at the desired activity.

- **Keep duplicates of popular toys.** Toddlers like to imitate their friends. It is one way they make friendship connections. So if you have several similar toys, for instance, toy shopping carts and hats, then the children can enjoy doing something together, rather than just waiting their turn.

- **Help the child learn to ask for a turn.** You can even give them words to say.

- **Help the child be heard.** Sometimes the asking child doesn't speak loud enough or is difficult to understand. Tell the other child, *"Molly, did you hear Max? He said he wants to ride the scooter when you're through. Okay?"*

- **Praise children for sharing a toy.**

Read a Book About Sharing and Act It Out

Materials

picture book about sharing or taking turns, such as *First Friends* by Lenore
    Blegvad or another on the list on page 91
some of the materials mentioned in the picture book you choose

To Do

Read the book to a small group of children. Talk about how the characters feel.
Help children notice the facial expressions on the characters in the book. Then
play a game of "let's pretend." *"Pretend you're this little boy in the book. Here, you
can hold the train like the one in the book."* Then read the book again and coach
the children to act out what is happening as you read it.

This allows the children to experience sharing or taking turns in an abstract
way. They are not emotionally involved. Later, when you notice children sharing
(or not), remind them of the similar scene in the book you read to them.

Homemade Book About Sharing

Materials

small photo album or zipper-closure bag book (see page 27)
camera

To Make

Photograph or draw a typical sharing sequence from your classroom. Children
might pose for you. It could be something like this: "Max Shares His Playdough."
Page 1: Max is poking some playdough. Page 2: Molly is sad because she doesn't
have any playdough. She looks at Max. Page 3: Max tears off a piece of his
playdough and gives it to Molly. Page 4: Max is smiling and Molly is smiling. They
are both happy because now they both have playdough.

Puppet Learns to Share

Materials

pet puppet
something to share, such as dry cereal, raisins, or crayons

To Do

Create a mini-drama in which your puppet is unhappy because either he
doesn't want to share something, or because someone will not share with him.
For instance, have Herkimer come out holding a box of raisins and announce:

Herkimer: *"I am happy, happy, happy, because my mommy gave me some raisins to eat."*

You: *"Oh, boy! We love raisins. Will you share some with us?"*

Herkimer: *"But they're mine! I want to eat them all myself!"*

You: *"Look at your friends' faces. They are sad because you are not sharing."*

Herkimer: *"Okaaaay…I guess you can all have some."*

Then have the puppet hand out several raisins to all of the children.

You: *"Look at their faces now, Herkimer. Everyone is happy. And guess what? We have something to share with you now. We will share our crayons with you and you can help us draw."*

Talk about how everyone feels.

Lots of Pieces, Lots of Sharing

Materials
any play material with lots of pieces, such as toddler-size Legos®, crayons, pegs, or a tub full of small cars

To Do
Encourage two or three children to "share" the material and play with it together or side by side at the same time. Bring your pet puppet over as they share and say to the puppet, *"See, Herkimer, these boys are sharing the cars. That's what sharing is. Sharing makes it even more fun to play with something."*

Variation
Outdoors, encourage children to share a bucket of water to "paint" the outside of the building. Give each child a large house-painting brush to dip into the water and spread on the walls.

Sharing a Space

Materials
large piece of butcher paper or a tabletop
fingerpaint

To Do
Tell the children that they can share the tabletop or butcher paper when they fingerpaint or scribble with crayons or markers. Notice how it's more fun to do something with friends and share the space. They could also share the water table or sensory table.

Puppet Learns to Take Turns

Materials
pet puppet
ball

To Do
Have the children sit in a circle and roll a ball back and forth while holding the puppet. When the ball comes to you, have the puppet hold onto it and not roll it back. The puppet can say, *"Well, this sure is boring, just sitting here with this ball."* Explain to the puppet, *"You don't understand, Herkimer. You have to take turns with the ball. That means that when you get the ball, you roll it to someone else. Then someone will roll it back to you and it will be your turn again. That way everyone can have fun with the ball and with each other."* Then make the puppet roll the ball away again and be overjoyed when he gets it back. He then demonstrates that he knows what to do. You can praise him, saying, *"Good, Herkimer! Now you know how to take turns. It's more fun, isn't it?"*

Practice Taking Turns in Circle Time

Materials
kitchen timer
small rug

To Do
Tell the children, *"We're going to take turns dancing today."* Have children take turns doing something, such as dancing to music on a "spotlight rug" while you set the timer for a very short time—30 seconds, if possible. Praise them when they sit down when the timer rings and let someone else dance.

Practice Taking Turns Outside

Materials

kitchen timer

popular riding toy

To Do

On the playground, announce to the children, *"We're going to practice taking turns with the scooter over here. Who wants to play with us?"* Then let the children play with the timer and see how it works. Let them help to set the timer when their friends ride the riding toy. Keep playing until everyone has had a turn. Children will need your participation and encouragement to take turns.

Puppet Narrations

Materials

pet puppet

To Do

Use the puppet to describe everything that is going on when successful sharing or taking turns is taking place. *"Wow…This is really interesting! Max and Molly are managing to play with this riding toy together. Look what is happening. Molly went up and asked Max for a turn. Max said, 'When I'm done.' Then Max rode around the circle one more time and got off. Then he helped Molly climb on. Now Molly is riding around the circle."* The puppet (or you, personally) could do this on the spot, later in circle time, or at the lunch table.

READ BOOKS ABOUT SHARING

Pat-a-Cake by Tony Kenyon. A toddler learns the fun of playing with someone else, and asks the baker for a cake to share with her baby sister.

Whoops! by Louise Batchelor. Two toddlers celebrate a birthday with their mothers while learning to share and use the words they know and enjoy.

Mine! by Miriam Cohen. Backpack Baby shows the possessions that belong to him that he is carrying on his walk. When he eats his pretzel he is very happy to share with his father.

Will I Have a Friend? by Miriam Cohen. Illustrated by Lillian Hoban. Jim is starting school, his very first day of kindergarten. His concerns about finding a friend are soon forgotten.

Sharing by Taro Gomi. Two little girls who are very good friends find interesting ways to divide things into equal parts to share.

Cleanup Time

When the room is disorganized and messy, children cannot play with as much concentration. They become even more easily distracted. There are times when everything must be put away and the room made neat. Before going outside is one of these times. If children come inside to a messy room, their play will be chaotic, and open playtime may not be next on your agenda. Also be sure the room is picked up before lunchtime so that the transition after lunch, before nap, and at the end of the day will go smoothly.

Surprisingly, cleanup time can be less troublesome in a toddler room than in a preschool classroom. The children can come to think of it as just a regular part of what we do here. In actuality, it will be the adults who do most of the cleaning up. Make your job easier by putting things away and cleaning up as the playtime continues rather than leaving everything out until it's actually cleanup time. Be conscious of your attitude. If you are cheerful and positive about putting things back into order rather than calling it a "mess," children are more likely to want to imitate you.

- **Let the puppet help.** Pet puppets make wonderful cleanup assistants. They can pick things up and hand them to a child who can put them into a box or on a shelf. Make sure puppets only help children who are actively involved in cleaning up. Because children want the attention of the puppet, they are likely to be eager to help clean up.

- **Put holes in the lids of storage boxes.** Store toys with many small pieces in a large box with a lid. Cut a hole in the lid. Toddlers love to stick things through holes. It will make putting toys away much more fun.

- **Have a picture of the toy on the storage container, and in the place where it is to be stored.** This helps children put things away in the correct container and in the proper place, making a fun matching game out of it.

- **Have extra cleaning cloths and sponges so children can imitate you.** Anything involving water, even a damp sponge, will draw the attention of toddlers. Cleaning off a tabletop can keep a toddler busy as an "activity" even before cleanup time starts.

Cleanup Music

Materials
recorded music
CD or cassette player

To Do
Find some peppy and fun instrumental music that you will use as a nonverbal signal for cleaning up. Marching band music is fun. Always play the very same music at cleanup time. Before long, as soon as the children hear the familiar music playing, they will start to put the toys away, with your help and encouragement.

Sing the Clean-Up Time Song

Sing this song to the tune of "I'm a Little Teapot."

> *Clean-up, clean-up,*
> *Clean-up time.*
> *Time to put*
> *The toys away,*
> *Time to put them*
> *On the shelf*
> *Because they won't go by themselves.*

To Do
Sing this over and over while you help children put things away. They can join you in the singing, and it provides children with another nonverbal signal that indicates what is expected.

Cleanup Time Sorting Game

Materials
one or more large laundry baskets

To Do
As you clean up, let the children toss all the toys on the floor into the laundry basket. Then, when everything is off the floor and in the basket, gather the children around. Take out one toy at a time and say, *"Who knows where this goes?"* Hand it to a volunteer and have everybody clap when she puts it in the correct place. Then go on to the next toy. You might allocate a little extra time to cleaning up this way—it is, after all, a very good cognitive activity. When everything has been put away, everybody claps and notices how nice the room looks. This works outside on the playground too.

Variation

Instead of a laundry basket, find something large on wheels such as a wagon or cart. Toddlers love things with wheels. They can help drag it from one place in the room to another as toys are tossed in.

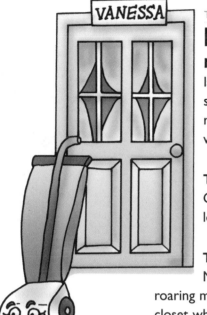

Pet Vacuum Cleaner

Materials
large wiggle eyes
super glue
red paint
vacuum cleaner

To Make
Glue the eyes on the vacuum cleaner and paint on red lips to make it look like a face.

To Do
Many toddlers are afraid of vacuum cleaners. This activity turns the roaring monster into a funny friend. You could also decorate the door to the closet where "Vanessa the Vacuum" is kept to look like a house. When the toys are picked up, or after any messy activity, you can say, "*It's time to feed Vanessa now. She's hungry.*" When you get Vanessa out of her "house," say, "*Vanessa is funny! She doesn't eat food like people do. She likes to eat the dirt on the floor and make our carpet clean for us.*" Some of the children will like a chance to push Vanessa around.

Inspection Train

To Do
When the room is fairly well picked up, start a "people train." Announce, "*Choo-choo! Get on the train to see if everything is clean.*" Chug around the room picking up passengers as you go. "*Yes, it's cleaned up here. You can get on the train.*" The train with all the passengers could end up in your story area or at the lunch table, or whatever comes next in your routine.

Homemade Books About Cleaning Up

Materials
small photo album or zipper-closure bag book (see page 27)
camera

To Make
Take a photo of the room when it is messy. Then photograph the children in various clean-up tasks. Finally, take a picture of everyone smiling and admiring

the nice, clean room. Arrange the photos in order and make simple captions. "Everybody Helps." Page 1: Our room was messy. Toys were everywhere. Page 2: Max lined up the trucks against the wall. Page 3: Molly wiped the table. Page 4: Jeremy put the Legos® in the box. Page 5: Miss Suzie swept the floor under the table. Last page: Now the room is nice and neat!

To Do
Read this book often to the children. They may want to talk about what they did that day that was different from what was pictured in the book. This will help build a sense of community—everyone works to get the job done—and a sense of pride.

Circle Time

To do, or not to do? That is the question. While circle time is a "staple" of preschool curriculum, it may not be a useful component in the toddler day. Be clear about why you are attempting this, and above all, keep it short, light, and easy. Perhaps you'll read a story. Maybe you'll pass out rhythm instruments to play lively music or pom-poms to dance with. The main benefit of having a large-group activity in which everybody gathers and does the same thing is not to develop language skills, as people sometimes think, but to develop a sense of community—to help children understand that they are a valued part of the group.

When you think about offering an activity during circle time, ask yourself if it really needs to be a circle time activity. Often it is better to do the activity with one or two children at a time. Singing and moving to music are examples of activities done best with the whole group.

- **Just start.** Rather than struggle to get all the children together, quiet, and paying attention to you, just flop down on the floor and start doing whatever it is you want to do with one or two children. The others are likely to gather automatically. If they don't, that's okay. They are still in the same room with you and will likely hear everything you say and benefit from what you are doing from afar.

- **Define the space well.** Spread a special quilt on the floor for children to sit on, or designate an area rug for this purpose.

- **Give each child a seat.** A small pillow or carpet square to sit on can help children stay put.

- **Make a picture seat.** Laminate pieces of construction paper, each with a child's photograph on it. Lay these on the floor where you want the children to sit. Each child must find his picture to know where to sit.

- **Create a small ritual.** Do the same types of things in the same order; perhaps a gathering song, followed by a greeting from the puppet, the treasure box activity, and a story. It's much easier for toddlers to participate if they feel they know what to expect.

- **Allow children to come and go.** Don't be upset if some of the children get up and wander away. If you pressure them to stay seated, circle time will quickly earn a negative reputation and the children will resist even more.

- **Create a songbook.** This helps you remember all the songs you have taught the children. On each page, put a picture that represents the song and the words to the song. Place the pages in a loose-leaf binder. Show the children the page and see if they can guess what song it is that they will be singing. Or, you could make loose cards in a similar way and place them in a file box. This is a good system to use with fingerplays, too.

- **Read it again, sing it again, do it again!** Toddlers love repetition of familiar things, probably because it gives them a feeling of mastery or control. If you have time, don't hesitate to repeat something you just did, especially if they ask for it.

- **Plan an orderly dismissal.** Rather than just stopping and letting children scatter into the room, have an orderly way to get them to the next activity. Your puppet could say the names of each child when it is time to wash their hands, put on coats, or whatever is next. Have one staff person ready to receive them in the new place.

TRANSITION ACTIVITY

Gathering Song

Come to the circle,
Come to the circle,
Come to the circle,
We'll have a little fun (or read a little book, or sing a little song, or play a little game).

To Do
Sit down on the floor, clap your hands in rhythm, and sing this to gather the children.

Shy Puppet

Materials

puppet

bag

To Do

Put the puppet in the bag. Shake the bag, as though someone is trembling inside. Look in and talk to the puppet. *"What's the matter, Herkimer?"* The puppet peeks out of the bag and then jumps back inside. Slowly bring the puppet out of the bag (on your hand) and make him continue to shake. Then he whispers something in your ear. By this time, children are usually quiet, straining to hear what the puppet is saying. *"He says he's afraid of all the noise out here. We'll be quiet for him, won't we?"* You might continue having the puppet whisper to you, or he can talk to the children in a timid voice, perhaps asking about what they did that morning, or what's going to happen next, or any other topic you have in mind.

Treasure Box or Blanket

Materials

large, fancy box or covered basket, or a fancy blanket to put over an object

To Do

Every day, put a different object into this box that can start your discussion with the children. Children will be eager to see what you have in the treasure box. Build some suspense as you open the lid. Then talk about whatever it is. It could be a clue, such as a wooden spoon, that indicates what you will do next. Or it could be something that is represented in a picture book you are going to read to the children. As soon as this box appears, children will gather automatically because it gives them another nonverbal signal.

Story Time

Your story time might take place during circle time, or it could be a special event, dedicated just to reading to children. Be sure to read to children at other times as well, as a spontaneous activity with one or two children before nap time or outside in the shade of a tree.

- **Wear a magic story hat.** Find a colorful, noticeable hat. Put this on whenever you are ready to read a story to children. The hat becomes a nonverbal signal and children will gather when they see it.

- **Have a well-organized book corner.** Find a bookshelf that allows you to display books so that the whole cover shows, rather than just the spine.

- **Limit the number of books.** Don't display every book you own. Select several for children to choose from and store the others. Change often, but leave favorites out.

- **Give children free access to books.** Books should be a choice during their playtime.

- **Teach children to respect books.** Show toddlers how to turn pages by using their thumb and forefinger rather than sliding their hand across the page. Promptly repair any tears.

- **Place stuffed animals in the book corner.** Encourage children to read to the animals.

TRANSITION ACTIVITY

"Read Me a Story" Song
Sing to the tune of "Down By the Station."

> Let's find a book and read a little story
> See the pretty pictures on each page.
> Each time we turn the page
> There's another picture.
> Oh, what fun!
> Let's read it again!

TRANSITION ACTIVITY

Story Time Activities

Materials
picture book
some of the items mentioned in the book you choose

To Do
After reading a picture book to the children, find something in the book that you can turn into an activity to end your story time. Are there interesting objects in the book, such as pots and pans? Find similar real objects for them to play with. Is there a food mentioned? Let them taste it. **Safety Note:** Check for food allergies. Is there an action, such as crossing a bridge? Encourage children to pretend to do that. With a little thought you can find an extension activity for almost any picture book. (See *Story S-t-r-e-t-c-h-e-r-s for Infants, Toddlers and Twos* by Shirley Raines, Karen Miller, and Leah Curry-Rood for a wealth of ideas.)

Story in a Can

Materials

large coffee can or other decorative tin with a lid
small props related to characters, objects, and events in
the story

To Do

Tell the children a simple story instead of reading it. (You
could "tell" the story of a picture book with which the
children are familiar.) As you tell the story, take objects or pictures out
of the can that represent that part of the story. Line them up. At the
end of the story, ask them about each prop. *"What was this in the story?"*
"Remember this one?" Then let the children play with the props. For instance, for
"Peter Rabbit" you might have three small bunnies, a blue coat, a small spade, a
watering can, and a bag of chamomile tea.

Avoid Large-Group Art and Cooking Activities

With the exception of short circle
time activities and music and
movement activities, avoid doing
activities with all of the children at
once. For example, doing art
activities as a large group is a recipe
for disaster because toddlers cannot
wait for others to get their smocks
tied and for materials to be handed
out. Usually, it doesn't take longer
to do activities with one or two
children at a time. If everyone who
wants to participate doesn't have a
chance to that day, offer it again
soon. The tips below also apply to cooking projects.

- **Gather all materials** ahead of time.

- **Invite one or two children** at a time to participate.

- **Talk.** Describe what the children are doing.

- **Relax.** Let children take their time.

- **Repeat.** If time allows, invite children to do it again. They'll
  gain even more from the activity.

- **Clean up.** When the child has finished, wash the child's hands and smock, if necessary.

- **Invite other children to participate.**

Dealing with "Herding"

One difficulty in working with very young children is that when you set up a special activity for just a few children at a time, they all crowd around and want to do it at the same time. It can be difficult, at first, to convince these children that they will have a turn when someone else is finished. This can also happen when there is a new toy that all children want to try or when any interesting activity begins. Crowding can lead to pushing, accidents, and tears.

Give the children constant reassurance that you will get them when it is their turn. In the meantime, make sure there are other interesting things to do while they wait. *"I know, Molly, it is really hard to wait when you really, really want to paint. I'll come and get you as soon as Max is through. Then it will be your turn. Why don't you build with the big blocks while you are waiting?"* Then, be true to your word. Find the child when it is her turn. Eventually the child will learn to trust you and can relax and play with something else in the meantime.

- **Divide into smaller groups.** One thing you have going for you is toddlers' distractibility. Pull some of the children in another direction by starting an activity in a different part of the room.

- **Create picture sign-ups.** Create a picture card for each child by laminating a photo. Place a waiting child's picture at the activity while he or she plays somewhere else. Having the picture there can make the child feel that they won't be forgotten. This works best with older children.

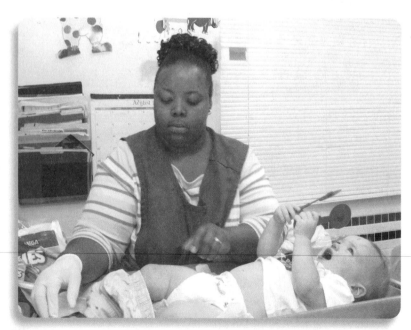

Diapering

The many times you diaper children each day all involve transitions. The first transition is when the child goes from playing to being diapered, being removed from "what's happening now" to lying on his back in a passive way as someone cleans him up. Next, there is the transition of hand washing. Finally, the child transitions back into the stream of activity.

In childcare centers, it is important for programs serving toddlers to have a low child/staff ratio because children might need diapering at any time. One adult can supervise the rest of the room while the other adult diapers a child. Programs have various ways of working this out. In some programs, a caregiver will only diaper the children for whom she is the primary caregiver. In most programs, any adult may diaper any child in the group. It is often a matter of who is deeply involved in supervising a messy project or conducting a group time or story time.

If you are working alone, that means you have a small group. When you are changing a child's diaper, offer the other children simple activity choices that don't require your close supervision.

Often, toddlers resist being diapered for many reasons. It's boring. They don't like being passive and instead, want to do everything themselves. The child may be deeply engaged in what he is doing and doesn't want to stop. Running away may be a child-invented game to engage your emotions. Finally, toddlers often resist doing what the adult wants just for the sake of resisting.

- **Try to avoid interrupting a child** who is deeply engaged in play. Wait a few minutes. "Deep play" is important.

- **Tell the child what you are going to do,** rather than just grabbing the child. Approach from the front. Hold your arms out if you intend to carry the child, or offer a hand if the child will walk.

- **State your intentions in a positive way** rather than posing a question. Instead of asking, *"May I change your diaper now?"* say, *"It's your turn, Molly. I'm going to change your diaper now."*

- **Give a positive choice.** If the child runs away or resists, ask, *"Do you want me to carry you, or would you rather walk by yourself?"*

- **Give the child some independence.** Arrange some steps so that the child can climb up to the diapering table by himself.

- **Try to make it fun.** Engage the child in conversation as you diaper him. Talk about what the child was doing, or what will happen next. You might have an interesting toy there for the child to hold.

- **Create a ritual** around hand washing. Do it together. Make soap gloves (see page 111). Make the most of this small one-on-one water playtime.

Toilet Learning

Learning to use the toilet is certainly a major life transition for both the child and the parents. Toddlers and two-year-olds are in the middle of this transition. Some children pick it up easily, while others seem to take forever. There is no "right age" when all children should be using the toilet. There are two major keys to success in toilet training children in a childcare center: 1) waiting until the child is developmentally ready and 2) having close communication and collaboration with parents. Learning to use the toilet should be a positive experience for the child.

The toilet training process really begins with diapering. Comments such as *"You are wet,"* or *"You have a poopy diaper,"* help children put language to this sensory experience. Additionally, upon seeing a child strain, the caregiver may question, *"Max, are you pooping in your diaper?"*

Some children are initially afraid of the toilet. The loud noise and the rushing water may startle them. Because the sound of flushing toilets is a common in a toddler childcare program, the child is likely to become accustomed to it. And the child's fear is likely to lessen as he sees other children successfully use the toilet in a matter-of-fact way. Indeed, the toilet becomes a fascinating thing to toddlers. They love the cause and effect of pushing the lever and seeing the water and contents go flushing down the hole. In fact, one of the major problems caregivers face is keeping children from flushing all manner of toys and other objects down the toilet. Children should be allowed to become familiar with the toilet and learn to flush it themselves. However, adults must supervise children closely.

Getting Together With Parents

Before beginning the toilet training process with any child, it is important to meet with the parents and any caregivers who will be involved in the process with the child. This meeting ensures that the toilet-training process is not taken casually and that everyone—caregivers, parents, and child—agree with the approach.

Write a description about how you teach children to use the toilet. Encourage the parents to use a similar method at home, for the sake of consistency. Your role is to encourage and support the parents in this process, and give them some insights into the child's readiness, and the process that helps children succeed. Agree ahead of time about the language you will use, and if little boys will stand or sit. Encourage the parent to start the process at home the weekend before you begin at the center.

Signs of Readiness

- The child tells you he or she is wet or needs the diaper changed.
- The child can pull clothes down and up.
- The child shows a strong interest.
- The child has good verbal communication skills. He needs to be able to tell you he needs to use the potty.
- The child can indicate when he is about to urinate or have a bowel movement.
- The child is dry at least two hours at a time or is dry after nap each day.

Some children resist toilet training simply because all the adults around them want them to do it. This is simply an indication that this child is finding out where his personal power is in this world. If you find a child offering a lot of resistance when you feel that he is otherwise ready, it's best to back off, or figure out a way to make the child think it is his idea. Often, it is the peer example that is the strongest motivator. When a child sees that many of his friends are using the toilet, he wants to feel like one of the gang and may finally agree to use the toilet. Sometimes, a comment from another child will have the strongest influence, such as *"I'm big now— I go potty."*

- **Leave the door open.** Do this so that the child can get to the toilet easily, whenever he needs to, and so that you can supervise easily. The child can also see other children using the toilet and will get the idea that this is the thing to do in this place.

- **Make it social.** Have the child go with a "buddy" for social reinforcement.

- **Use cloth underpants.** Ask the parents to put the child in regular cloth underpants rather than pull-ups or training pants. Pull-ups are so absorbent that the child may not feel uncomfortable when wet.

- **Provide extra clothing.** Ask parents to bring several changes of clothing, including socks and shoes. (Also have an extra supply of old clothing at the center, in case you run out.) It is important that the child feels really wet in order for him to get the idea that using the toilet is a much better idea.

- **Create some regular times in your daily schedule** when everyone who is potty trained is encouraged to use the toilet. Before going outside and before naps are especially important.

- **Allow children who aren't yet potty trained to watch if they are curious.** It is part of their learning process.

- **Be there to help.** Even when children are completely toilet trained, they may still need assistance with wiping and dressing.

- **Supervise the bathroom** closely and do not allow children to play there.

- **When toileting accidents happen don't show disapproval.** Simply help the child clean up in a matter-of-fact way and reassure him that it's okay.

- **Be sure to make hand washing a routine activity after toileting** (see pages 110-111).

Managing Toilet Training While Everything Else Is Going On

When you start the toilet training process with a child, he will need a lot of support and many reminders. Take the child to the toilet every 30–45 minutes during the first few weeks. Perhaps one staff person could be in charge of this, while the other concentrates on what is happening in the play area. The child must know that he can go to the toilet at any time. You need to be able to supervise the toilet area easily, and children will probably need help wiping, pulling up clothing, and washing hands afterwards.

For children who are already toilet trained, it makes sense for toileting to be going on while other children are being diapered at regular times in the routine, such as before going outside and before naptime.

Cultural Issues Around Toilet Training

Every family has its own traditions and language around this issue. Often, emotions run high. In some cultures, children are "trained" very early. Some methods, such as putting the child on a potty every 10 minutes, or making the child sit on the potty for long periods of time are not possible in group care.

Accidents Will Happen

Naturally, there will be accidents when the child doesn't make it to the toilet on time. Deal with these in a matter-of-fact way without criticism. In both the process of diapering and helping children with the toilet, avoid all negative comments (and guard your facial expressions, as well). Give encouragement—*"That's okay…maybe next time you'll remember to use the toilet."* Reinforce success with praise. It is really a major accomplishment!

READ BOOKS ABOUT TOILET LEARNING

Everyone Poops by Taro Gomi
Koko Bear's New Potty by Vicki Lansky
Once Upon a Potty by Alona Frankel
Going to the Potty by Fred Rogers

Outside Time

Most toddlers love playing outside where they can run, shout, and climb to their hearts' content. Unless the weather is severe, all young children benefit greatly from active outside playtime every day. Adjust your outdoor time according to your local climate. In hot climates, you will want to go outside earlier in the morning and later in the afternoon. In cold climates, enjoy outdoor times as close as possible to noon.

The process of getting ready to go outside includes a number of transitions. All children should be freshly diapered or given a chance to use the toilet so that you will not have to come back inside sooner than you planned. Most times of the year, you won't just be able to open the door and walk outside. Children will need some sort of outer clothing. Children should also wear sunscreen and hats.

🡇 **Divide the group.** If you have a large group and there is adequate staff to maintain required staff/child ratios in both places, consider sending half of the children outside while the others play indoors. Then switch. Toddlers always do better in smaller groups.

🡇 **Minimize waiting time.** Between diapering, toileting, and dressing, some waiting time may develop for those children who are ready first. This can create unrest because toddlers hate to wait. If possible, have one adult go outside with a group of children who are ready and then, if your room has an exit door directly onto the playground, send out other children one at a time when they are ready. Waiting is especially difficult if children have warm clothing on, such as snowsuits.

🡇 **If necessary, plan a waiting activity.** If waiting is absolutely unavoidable, make it as short as possible and have something interesting for the children to do while they wait. One good idea is to have a basket of old greeting cards for them to look through. Only give these to them during this brief transition so their interest will remain high. Or, simply give each child a loop of masking tape on his index finger. That should buy you five minutes.

🡇 **Watch for overcrowding.** Remember toddlers' instinct for herding, that is, everyone wants to do the same thing at the same time. Be there to divert some children into another activity.

🡇 **Parallel play with the children.** Follow their lead and do what they are doing. You can then add a little variety or depth to what is going on. While you are doing this though, keep an eye and ear on the rest of the playground so you can be alert to when you are needed elsewhere.

🡇 **Plan for richness and variety.** Regard your outdoor play area as another rich activity area of your classroom. One automatically thinks of gross motor activities outside, such as playing with balls or a parachute. You can really do almost anything outside that you can do inside, but some things are easier and better to do outside. Very active, noisy, or messy activities can be better outside. Don't forget to provide for pretend play. Outside is the ideal place for a rhythm band parade. Water play poses fewer problems in this location. Now is the time to run and pretend to fly. You might even have them practice their loud "outside voices." Pots and pans from your housekeeping corner are great enrichments for the sand box. Hats, capes, and other dress-up clothes are fun on the playground as well.

- **Plan for hygiene outside.** Bring a box of tissues and a plastic bag for used tissues. Some moist wipes can be handy. A water cooler and some paper cups are advisable if you don't have an outdoor drinking fountain.

- **Supervise toileting.** Do the best you can to ensure that every child goes to the bathroom before you go outside. However, if a child must go to the bathroom, do not send him back into the room alone. It is easy for a child to slip out of the bathroom and wander through the rest of the building or even out onto the street. So, if a child needs to go to the bathroom, you'll have to take at least part of the group back inside, depending on how many staff can remain on the playground to supervise the others.

- **Prepare children to go back inside.** As with other transitions throughout the day, children need advance notice before it is time to return to the classroom. Tell them, *"In a few minutes we will be going back inside."* Talk about what will happen once you are inside.

- **Have a cleanup time outside.** Let children drive their riding toys into the shed. Have children help you collect sand toys and put them in a storage container. Do this even if you will be coming back outside later in the day. It is much more pleasant to come outside to a picked up play yard rather than one that is strewn with toys.

TRANSITION ACTIVITY

The Old Coat Trick

To Do

Place the child's coat on the floor in front of her, zipper-side up, collar near her feet. Have the child put one hand in each armhole, and then flip the coat up over her head.

Song About Putting on Coats

Sing to the verse tune of "Oh, Susanna."

> *First one arm,*
> *Then the other,*
> *Then we go flip, flip, flip.*
> *First one arm,*
> *Then the other,*
> *Now we go zip, zip, zip (or button, button, button).*

Song About Going Outside

Make up a song while you're getting children dressed to go outside. Squeeze your lyrics into any melody. Continue to make up lines about children's possible activities. Don't worry if it doesn't rhyme. Here is an example:

> *What will you do when you go outside?*
> *Will you play on the swings, will you slide down the slide?*
> *Will you dig in the sand*
> *Or run in the wind?*
> *I can't wait to see.*
>
> *Max says he will climb up high*
> *Until he can almost reach the sky.*
> *Molly will push the shopping carts,*
> *And Zane might ride a bike*
> *And stop and start.*

A Walking Rope

Materials

long piece of clothesline

To Make

Tie a knot in the clothesline about every 18 inches.

To Use

Have each child hold onto a knot with one hand (make sure children are facing in the same direction!). Then go for short walks, with everyone holding onto a knot on the rope. Toddlers like this activity. The rope and the knot give them something definite to hold onto, and they love playing "train." It can be a pleasant way to keep children together on a walk. If possible, have an adult at both ends of the line. Walk in the neighborhood or practice just walking around the playground.

What Do You See in the Sky?

Lie on your backs in the grass and look at the sky while you recite this poem
(remember to improvise!).

Look at the sky, way up high —
What is that you see?
I see a cloud floating by
As fluffy as it can be.

I see a bird flying around
And landing in a tree.
Airplane! Airplane! There it goes,
Saying goodbye to me.

Listening Cards

Materials

index cards
pictures of objects found outside that make sounds

To Make

Make picture cards of common objects that make sounds, such as a car, a truck,
birds, grasshoppers, frogs, airplanes, garbage trucks, or anything else you are
likely to hear outside. Recite the following poem:

Listen, listen, what do you hear?
What's that sound?
Is it far?
Is it near?

Then let the children find the picture that represents the sound. Have blank
cards for new sounds. Write what the sound is and find a picture later.

Get on the Train

Sing this song to the tune of "Down By the Station."

Get on the train, let's go for a ride,
Get on the train, it's time to go inside.
Around to the door…we're almost there now.
Stomp, stomp, shake, shake,
Here we are!

Make a "people train" and start out with a loud "toot, toot!" and some chugging
sounds to entice the children to join you. Repeat the first two lines until
everybody is "on board," and repeat the "stomp, stomp, shake, shake" line while
you brush any sand, leaves, grass, or dirt off the children.

Hand Washing

One of the drawbacks of group care for children is an increased exposure to germs. The best defense against it is frequent and thorough hand washing. Children and adults should wash hands before eating, after diapering and toileting, and after blowing their noses or participating in other messy activities. Because toddlers love water play, you probably won't have much trouble involving them in this activity.

🔖 **Create a ritual.** Make hand washing such a regular part of the lunchtime and diapering routine that children think it is strange and unusual not to do so.

🔖 **Build independence.** Adjust your environment so that the children can do the whole hand-washing procedure independent of adult help. It might mean adding a stable step in front of the sink so children can reach the faucets. Adjust the temperature on the water heater so that there is no possibility of children scalding themselves. Teach the children how to turn the faucets on and off.

🔖 **Keep soap handy.** Put a bar of soap inside a cut-off leg of a pair of pantyhose and tie it to the faucet, or near the sink where children can reach it. This prevents much of the mess. You may also use liquid soap in a dispenser.

🔖 **Rinse off germs.** Make sure children rinse their hands thoroughly.

🔖 **Plan ahead.** Bring disinfecting hand-washing liquids or towelettes with you outside, or when you know you'll be away from convenient hand-washing places.

TRANSITION ACTIVITY

Washing Hands Ritual

To Do

After the diaper is changed, wash your hands and the child's hands. This can be a little ritual you share. Holding your hands under running water, you can sing (to the tune of "Here We Go 'Round the Mulberry Bush"):

This is the way we wash our hands,
And rub our hands, and scrub our hands.
This is the way we wash our hands.
Now they're nice and clean.
All done!

Hand Massage

Materials

lotion

To Do

After the child has clean hands, use the lotion to give him a gentle hand and arm massage. This loving activity feels good at any time of day!

Soap Gloves

Materials

soap

running water

To Do

Show the child how to rub the soap into a creamy lather that covers his hands like gloves. Then, show him how to rinse the lather off thoroughly. This activity helps to ensure that the child washes hands thoroughly enough. After children are familiar with this, remind them to "put their soap gloves on" when they wash their hands.

Homemade Book About Washing Hands

Materials

small photo album or zipper-closure bag book (see page 27)

camera

To Make

Photograph a child doing all the steps of hand washing. Arrange the photos in order and create simple captions. "Clean Hands for Molly." Page 1: Molly has been digging in the sand. Her hands are dirty. Page 2: Molly turns on the faucet. Page 3: Molly gets her hands wet. Page 4: Molly rubs soap on her hands. Page 5: Molly makes soap gloves. Page 6: Molly rinses the soap off of her hands. Page 7: Molly dries her hands with the paper towel. Page 8: Now Molly's hands are nice and clean.

Lunchtime

Children can become a little keyed up at lunchtime. Food is important. The children are hungry and perhaps a little bit cranky and tired after a full morning of play. Make sure that there is a dependable routine for this part of the day. Use lunchtime as the start of a quieting down time in preparation for nap time.

- **Get help.** Let "helper" children help you wipe off the tabletop. They can use a spray bottle with water in it and a clean cloth or sponge.

- **Be prepared.** Don't bring the children over to sit at the lunch table until the food is there.

- **Seat children at the same place each day.** Eliminate some of the stress at the beginning of lunchtime by teaching children exactly where to sit.

- **Be a social director.** Always sit down at the table and eat lunch with the children. Be a good role model. Talk about the delicious food in front of you and name what is on their plates. Also talk about what you did that morning. You are giving them language in a meaningful context and creating a pleasant atmosphere around the lunch table.

- **Anticipate spills.** Have a sponge or cleaning cloth ready and available to clean up spills. Don't make a big deal out of accidental spills. Either calmly wipe it up yourself or let the child do it. (Be careful not to turn this into a fun "activity" so that the children will purposely spill something so that they get to wipe it up.) The less attention you give it, the better.

- **Anticipate nap time pleasantly.** Reinforce the idea that resting is pleasant and good. *"Ah...soon we will be able to stretch out on our cots and snuggle in with our blankets and our loveys, and it will feel sooooo good!"*

- **Teach children to scrape plates.** Put out a few plastic dish tubs. Show children how to scrape their leftover food into one; put their plate, cup, and fork into another; and put their napkins into the wastebasket. Even if this takes a little longer than doing it all yourself, it is good to build this sense of independence in the children.

- **Use washcloths for a quick hand and face wipe.** Dampen a stack of clean washcloths with warm water. When children are finished scraping their plates, they can pick up a washcloth from the top of the stack and wipe their own faces and hands, and then put the used washcloth in a separate tub. Hint: Use identical washcloths of the same color because toddlers tend to want, and fight over, the item that seems "special."

TRANSITION ACTIVITY

Find Your Own Chair

Materials
photographs of children
clear self-adhesive paper

To Make
Affix the photos to the backs of the chairs using the clear self-adhesive paper.

To Do
Introduce this by playing a game with the children. Line up all of the chairs. Go to each chair and ask the children to say whose it is by looking at the picture. Then mix up the chairs and let them find their own chairs and sit down. Do this several times, putting the chairs in a different order each time. (This game will remain available to you anytime you need to fill a few moments.) Put the chairs at the lunch table and let children find their own chairs. Place children strategically, without being obvious. Toddlers often fight over chairs, especially if they are different colors or styles. This idea eliminates that conflict, and children will develop a feeling of ownership about their own chairs.

Table-Setting Templates

Materials
construction paper
clear self-adhesive paper

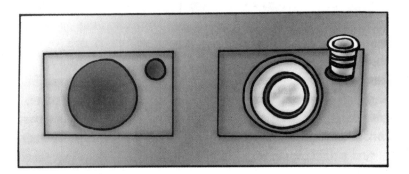

To Make
On construction paper, trace around the shapes of plates and cups that the children use and cut them out. Place these in position on the table and cover each with clear, self-adhesive paper. It is typical for toddlers to put their cup or drinking glass right next to the edge of the table, often causing spills, so put the circle for the cup towards the middle of the table.

To Do
Introduce this by letting all of the children help you set the table. Turn it into a matching game. *"Put the plate on the big circle like this. Good! Now put the cup on the little circle."* Each day, let one or two children help you set the table. As you eat lunch with the children, remind them to put their cup back on its circle.

Do-It-Yourself Bib

Materials
terrycloth hand towels or kitchen towels
cotton ribbing available at fabric stores

To Make
Cut a hole in the towel for the child's head to fit through. Sew cotton ribbing around the hole.

To Do
Show the child how to put on his own bib. Then hand out bibs at the lunch table and let the children put their bibs on together. They will like doing the same thing as all of their friends and will gain a feeling of independence.

Transition From Lunch to Nap

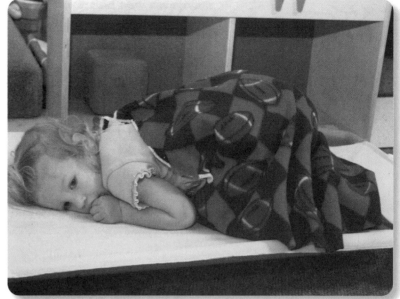

This is acknowledged as the most difficult transition of the day. There is much to do. If your program is fortunate enough to have "floater" staff, or if an extra pair of hands is available from administrative or volunteer staff, this is a good time to ask for help. Most likely, you will need to:

- Get dishes back to the kitchen.
- Clean up the lunch area— clean off tabletops and wipe with disinfecting solution.
- Clean off chairs, if necessary.
- Sweep and mop the floor.
- Set out cots, sheets, blankets.
- Accomplish diapering and toileting.
- Wash hands, both yours and children's, after diapering or toileting.
- Settle the children down to sleep.

To make this time go smoothly, have clear staff roles assigned—who puts out cots, who supervises toileting, who does diapering, who cleans up the lunch area, and so on. Do what you can to streamline these tasks. One caregiver can leave the lunch table early to put out cots and then be available to start diapering children who have finished eating and are ready. Another person might be in charge of supervising toileting and hand washing as the lunch area is cleaned. Children can get their security items from their cubbies. Both staff can then settle children down for nap time. The exact division of labor will depend on several things, such as room arrangement and the number of children requiring diapering.

Diapering and Toileting Before Nap Time

Every child should use the toilet or have on a dry diaper at the beginning of nap time. Although you don't want to rush children, and assembly line diapering and toileting is never a good idea, this is not the time for the lingering and tender interactions you might have with children when you diaper them at other times. See pages 102-105 for a discussion of toilet learning.

🖐 **Start early.** One staff person can start the diapering as soon as the first child is ready to leave the table.

- **Supervise well.** Station one staff person near the bathroom to supervise and help children with clothing and hand washing.

- **Keep track.** Create a reusable checklist to make sure that you have diapered children and washed their hands.

- **Tuck in.** Children who have been diapered or have used the bathroom can settle on their cots with their security items. You might give each child an initial "tuck-in" after diapering or toileting before going to the next child.

- **Give waiting children something to do.** A small basket of books and stuffed animals could be available for those who have left the table and are waiting to be diapered.

Nap Time

This much-needed daily transition gives both children and staff a chance to refuel. You are less likely to have problems getting children to sleep than preschool teachers, because toddlers still need a great deal of sleep. Remember that, even when all of the children are asleep, the nap room needs constant supervision.

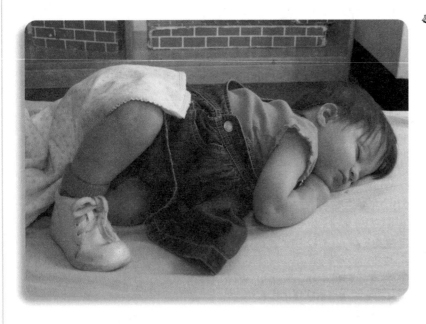

- **Set cots or mats out in an established pattern.** Put each child's cot or mat in exactly the same place each day. This gives the child a sense of security. First of all, he can easily find his own cot. Secondly, it is easier to slip off to sleep if the "scenery" is the same from day to day. Have a diagram on the wall to remind yourself or any substitute staff of the pattern. Each child's cot or mat, of course, should be labeled. Spread out each child's blanket on his temporary bed to welcome him.

- **Cots are a signal.** Do not set out cots until this time, after lunch, or at most, during the lunchtime. One staff person could leave the lunch table a few minutes early to accomplish this task. Since toddler groups are small, it should not take long. (In some centers, cots are set out as early as mid-morning when children come inside from outdoor play, filling up the room. Not only does this inhibit play and give any visitor the wrong impression about what goes on in the classroom, but also caregivers lose the opportunity to give children another nonverbal transition signal.) When children see the cots all spread out and ready right after lunch, they are more likely to get themselves "in the mood" for sleep.

- 🐾 **Darken the room.** Pulling down the curtains, darkening the room in other ways, and turning off the lights are more nonverbal signals that tell children it is time to sleep.

- 🐾 **Have special books for nap time.** Read books softly and slowly to children before they settle down on their cots. Then, as you tuck them in, you can refer to the book. "Now you can settle in, just like Little Bear (or any other character) did in the book."

- 🐾 **Play soft music.** Again, this is a nonverbal signal. Find some soothing music to play, and play the same selection each day as children settle down on their cots or mats.

- 🐾 **Tuck in children individually.** Tuck in those children who show they are "ready" when they lie on their cots quietly.

- 🐾 **Give puppet kisses.** Use the pet puppet to kiss them goodnight.

- 🐾 **Give back rubs.** Some children enjoy settling down with a short back rub.

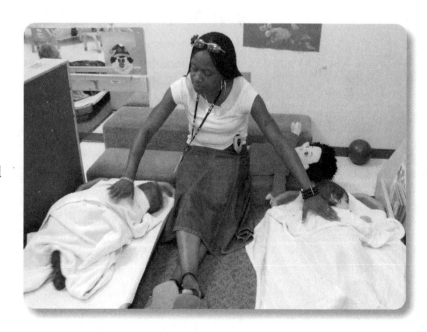

- 🐾 **Whisper.** Be calm. Be boring. Breathe deeply. Move slowly. Yawn.

- 🐾 **Sing.** Sing each child a personal lullaby including his name (see "Lullaby" on the next page or make up your own).

- 🐾 **Use security objects.** Most children settle down more easily with their security item at this time.

Very Tired Puppet

Materials

pet puppet

To Do

Do this at the lunch table or in a very short group time after diapering and toileting (although some of the children might be asleep by then.) The puppet could come out to talk to the children and tuck them in. Make the puppet keep yawning. There is nothing as contagious as a yawn. You might even get the children to yawn along with the puppet. This can really help them settle down.

Lullaby

Sing this song to the tune of "Twinkle, Twinkle Little Star."

> *Close your eyes, oh Molly, dear,*
> *It's time to take a rest right here.*
> *Dream a dream of all the play*
> *That you've done with us today.*
> *Close your eyes, oh Molly, dear,*
> *It's time to take a rest right here.*

Magic Sleep Spray

Materials

spray bottle
lightly scented water (such as lavender water)

To Do

After you tuck each child in, spray a little of the lightly scented water over each cot. Say, *"Here's a little bit of sleep spray to help you have good dreams."* This might become just one more part of your regular ritual to help children settle down.

READ BOOKS ABOUT NAPTIME

If You Were My Bunny by Kate McMullan. Illustrated by David McPhail. Loving lullabies to baby animals can be sung to common tunes. The final song is from a mama to her baby.

No Nap by Eve Bunting. It's Susie's naptime, but Susie isn't tired. "No nap," she says. So dad makes his own plans to tire Susie out. A fresh and humorous approach to naptime.

Goodnight Moon by Margaret Wise Brown. A classic among books for young children. This is a perfect book to read before nap or bedtime.

Max's Bedtime by Rosemary Wells. Max can't go to sleep. Ruby tries everything but Max wants his red elephant. A humorous ending as Max falls out of bed and finds the elephant, and Ruby falls into his bed, exhausted from trying to get him to sleep.

Baby's Goodnight Book by Kay Chorao. This is a Lap Library book in sturdy board format. A beautifully illustrated collection of favorite lullabies for nap or bedtime.

The Napping House by Audrey and Don Wood. "There is a house, a napping house, where everyone is sleeping." An infectious, humorous, cumulative rhyming story. Children will giggle and chuckle all the way to bed. The board edition is perfect for toddlers to hold.

The Going to Bed Book by Sandra Boynton. For little ones reluctant to go to bed, sometimes a silly book is just the thing. Sandra Boynton is the queen of silly books and toddlers love them!

When Children Don't Nap

Sometimes children, especially when new to the program, are just too tense or fearful to nap. Do all of the consistent, quieting activities listed above. The child must develop trust in you to allow himself to slip off to sleep. Make sure that the rest of the environment is quite boring, with nothing interesting to lure him away.

If, after about 15 or 20 minutes of lying quietly on his cot or mat the child truly cannot go to sleep, the child should be allowed to get up and play quietly somewhere else, preferably in a different room. Children will still benefit from this rest. It is close to torture to force a child to lie still in a darkened room when he cannot sleep. Children have varying energy levels and different personal sleeping and waking rhythms.

It is very difficult for young children to play quietly. Some possibilities for quiet play are: rubber puzzles, playdough, or looking at picture books. They will probably still vocalize—it's very hard for a toddler to whisper.

Waking Up

Don't forget the importance of this transition. While some children may wake up full of energy and "ready to go," most make a more gradual transition from the subconscious to the conscious state.

Should you allow children to sleep as long as they like, or should you wake them up after a certain amount of time? As other children start to wake up, the lights go on, and activity in the room resumes, most children will awaken on their own. While you want to remain flexible, most

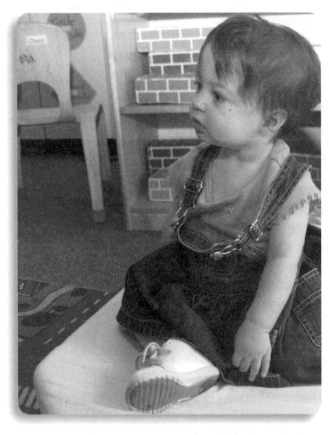

children should probably be awakened after sleeping about two hours. Parents generally appreciate a child who is ready to go to bed at a reasonable hour. Sometimes children will just naturally require more sleep than they usually do, when they didn't sleep well the night before, or when they are recovering from an illness, for instance. Talk to the parents about this. If a child really does need more sleep at this time of day, perhaps there is a quiet place in the room where the child could continue slumbering.

- **Create a gentle, slow "re-entry" time**. Give the waking child a hug and some cuddling if he seems to want it.

- **Bring the child to the bathroom or change a diaper.**

- **Have quiet activities set out.**

- **Eventually, turn the lights on** (at the same time each day) and start to fold blankets and put cots or mats away.

- **Serve an afternoon snack when children wake up.** Snack time is a good way to "re-enter" the classroom activities. The children might be hungry and dehydrated. Healthy snack food can help children gain renewed energy for play. It also gives them a chance to reconnect socially.

The Afternoon

Your afternoon should not be very different from the morning. You will have the same segments of routine—snack, inside play, outside play, and so on, but each segment will be shorter in length. For that reason, you might want to plan activities that are easier to clean up or are less complex. Keep in mind that your afternoon should be just as "educational" and rich in experiences as the morning.

- **Change something.** Give your environment a fresh aspect. You might put out a different choice of sensory play, or highlight different toys.

When Waiting Is Unavoidable

Even with the best of planning, there may be times when you need to occupy children for a few minutes. Every experienced teacher has simple activities to pull out at a moment's notice to keep boredom at bay. Here are some possibilities:

- Sing songs.
- Do fingerplays.
- Create an apron with many small pockets in it. Place small toys in the pockets for the children to discover and play with.
- Hide a music box and let children search for it while it is playing.
- Give children a box of old greeting cards to look at.
- Provide stickers for the children.
- Give each child a loop of masking tape on his finger.
- Play with pipe cleaners (chenille stems).
- Bring out a collection of pretty napkin rings.
- Roll a ball back and forth in a circle.
- Look through the family photos book with the children.
- Use a magnet board. Put magnetic self-stick backing on pictures for variety.
- Place contact paper low on a wall, sticky side out, with interesting things to stick to it near outside door.
- Have a box of clear plastic shaker bottles and plastic tubes with interesting things inside.
- Provide new books to enjoy.

Behavior Transitions

The transition from playing peacefully to aggressing against others can come quickly in a group of toddlers. While toddlers want very much to have friends and get along with other children, they still see the world purely from their own point of view. Because they are just beginning to learn the niceties of verbal give and take, it is more common for toddlers to act out physically, by hitting, kicking, biting, and so on. When frustrations build, tantrums are common for some children. Crying and whining are normal for others. Caregivers for toddlers spend much of their time coaching children through their conflicts. There are some things you can do to reduce this behavior.

- **Care for toddlers in small groups.** Even when child/staff ratios are ideal, aggression increases when toddlers are in large groups. There are more bodies to compete with, they are more easily distracted and overwhelmed, and frustration builds.

- **Have at least two adults in the room.** It is easier to see tension building and intervene when at least one adult is free to survey the whole group while the other concentrates on one child or an activity.

- **Look at room arrangement.** Avoid over-crowding children. Separate active activities from quiet activities. Create cozy nooks and crannies.

- **Intervene before the situation is critical.** Sometimes you can feel tension rising in the room. Start something new. Give them a change of scene—even a walk down the hall and back. Change the pace. Play some music. Plop down on the floor with a couple of books.

- **Distract and redirect.** When inappropriate behaviors begin, quickly get something else going. Either distract them with something totally different, or redirect them to the closest legitimate activity, such as throwing balls instead of sand.

- **Stay close to aggressors.** You know the children who have a shorter fuse. Position yourself near them, play with them, and be there to encourage positive behaviors when they are faced with a challenge.

- **Be a model.** Children learn behaviors from the important adults in their lives. When they are treated with understanding and gentle kindness they are more likely to develop this style themselves.

Starting Over

The transition from being out of control and removed from the group to back in the group often requires skillful assistance from caregivers. When you have had to enforce limits on a child, by removing him from the group briefly, forbidding an activity, and coaching him with love and gentle guidance to choose more positive behaviors, you need to rebuild the relationship between you and the child.

- **Start something different.** When the child returns to the group, direct him to something quite different from what he was doing before the incident occurred. Sensory play is often a good choice. It is soothing and doesn't require too much social give and take.

- **Spend some one-on-one playtime with the child.** This can be difficult to do when you are upset with the child and your nerves are on edge. But it is time well spent—for both of you. You need to re-establish a friendly relationship. If the child thinks you don't like him anymore, he may stop trying to get along and instead, his angry behaviors may increase. Play with cars and trucks together, dig in the sand, or play with playdough to let the child feel that he has good ideas and that you like to be with him. Now is not the time to lecture about his past behavior.

🐾 **Catch the child doing something right.** Find something positive to praise so the child senses that you still like him.

Dealing With Tantrums

These emotional meltdowns of toddlerhood cause a major disruption in your day. A screaming, out-of-control child can be a danger to other children and to himself, and certainly can make it difficult to carry on with planned activities. It becomes easier if you have a standard way of handling these outbursts.

🐾 **Prevent when possible.** You might become aware of what situations trigger tantrums in certain children and be able to avoid them. Just keeping children happily occupied in interesting play activities can help.

🐾 **Don't buckle.** While it may be tempting to give in and give the child what he wants in order to stop the outburst, this simply teaches the child that this handy technique works. Don't reinforce this negative behavior.

🐾 **Offer empathy.** Let the child know you "feel his pain." *"I know it's hard to wait your turn when you really, really want something. I will help you wait."*

🐾 **Create a place.** Have a standard place (not their cot or mat) that is easy to supervise where you put children to have their tantrums. Have some large pillows there and other soft things. Do not make this a place that is singled out for isolation. Use the area for other things, as well.

🐾 **Separate the child from the group.** Bring the child to the space just described and say, *"You can be over here with these soft things until you feel better and are ready to be with us again. We'll be over there."* The child may learn to come over by himself, and you can welcome him back, or you might go over and invite him. *"Do you think you have cried long enough? We'd like to have you back with us again."*

🐾 **Offer water.** Sometimes offering the child a glass of water after he has carried on for a while helps him to calm down.

- **Go for a walk.** Perhaps you can arrange it so that you can take the child by the hand and go for a brief walk outside of the classroom, just to allow the child to regroup. Don't use this time to lecture the child.

- **Help the child "re-enter"** as described above.

- **Stay calm.** Above all, put on your serenity face. Don't mirror the child's emotions and escalate the outburst.

Bad-Weather Activities

Days when weather keeps you inside can be very difficult. It is then when we really appreciate the benefits of outdoor play for children. The secret to surviving spells of bad weather is to develop a separate set of activities that you do *only* during the time when children would ordinarily be outside— preferably activities that give the same type of benefit to the child that outdoor play can offer. What are these benefits? We'll consider them here and offer some suggestions.

Offer a Change of Scenery

Different views can be refreshing. A child who is having difficulties in one place can leave the problem behind when the view changes. What are some ways you could change the scene for the 45 minutes you would be outside?

- **Go for a walk.** Bring out your "walking rope" (see page 108) and go for a walk inside your center. Walk up and down the halls and in and out of other classrooms, if possible.

- **Trade spaces.** Could you switch classrooms with another class that cannot go outside, giving both groups a change of scenery for a short segment of time?

- **Gym time.** Some centers are fortunate enough to have a gross motor room or gym where the children can play.

- **Make caves.** Use boxes and blankets to create tunnels and caves. Add a flashlight for even more fun.

- **Bring out special equipment.** Keep certain pieces of gross motor equipment separate for indoor use only, and only when you cannot go outside. Push furniture aside, if necessary, to make room to use this equipment. There are many possibilities, which you can vary from time to time, such as a parachute, one or more tunnels, a large collection of all kinds of balls, a low climber and slide, gym mats, indoor riding toys, and so on. The key is to keep them special.

- **Make a train with chairs.** This seems to be a never-fail activity with toddlers. They sometimes create this spontaneously, but will always love it when someone else initiates it. Add dolls, stuffed animals, and sound effects. Sing "The Wheels on the Bus."

- **Make stocking balls.** Cut off the legs of a clean pair of old pantyhose or tights. Tie a knot in one end of a leg. Stuff in a large handful of stuffing material and tie another knot directly over it. Then cut below the knot. Tie another knot and repeat. You should be able to get about six "balls" from each leg.

Encourage Loud Voices and Deep Breathing

Get that blood circulating to the brain! Loud voices require deep breathing. Getting children to be loud is not the problem—it's quieting them down again that requires patience.

- **Play noisy games,** such as pretending to be airplanes. Ask the children to roar and soar and then turn off their engines.

- **Teach them to whisper**—a new and fascinating game for toddlers.

- **Inflate.** Games that encourage children to pretend to be balloons and float around with their arms spread help them breathe deeply.

- **Play parachute games.**

- **Stretch.** Model various stretches. The children will love to imitate you.

Sensory Play

Children love to play with sand and water outdoors. Offer some cool, moist, soothing material in your sensory table for this time of the day. Clay is ideal.

TRANSITION ACTIVITY

Bad-Weather Fun Box

Materials

large, decorated box

variety of special materials such as manipulatives they have not used recently, Legos®, puzzles, containers of different shapes and sizes with lids and some with handles (not all at the same time)

covered shoebox with some "treasures" inside such as colored clothespins, material to feel, or a small stuffed animal or doll

discovery bottles (plastic bottles with various things inside to shake around)

kitchen utensils and plastic bowls

grooming objects such as combs, toothbrushes, and small washcloths

colorful scarves

crayons with sparkles

sensory books, such as the Dorling Kindersly books

To Do

Take advantage of the novelty factor to revive children's focus and attention. Take out this special box only at this time. Change its contents occasionally.

End of the Day

It is not uncommon for the quality of childcare to deteriorate in the late afternoon. Many teachers of young children complain about this time of the day when everyone seems to fall apart. The children, and maybe even the adults, can be tired and cranky. The room might be a mess. Sometimes inexperienced staff is working at this time. And this is when parents start to come to pick up children. Instead of seeing you at your best, they may see you at your worst. The following tips are gleaned from caregivers who have planned ahead, anticipating this time.

🥄 **Offer a late afternoon juice snack.** Children may become cranky and out of sorts if they are dehydrated. A snack of 100% juice (not sugar water), and perhaps a bit of protein such as cheese cubes can do wonders. Plus, just sitting at the table quietly eating can be rejuvenating and can help children refocus.

- **Limit your environment.** You will probably want to close off certain areas of your room that tend to be quite messy, such as the block center or the sensory table, and not put out toys with lots of small pieces. However, it's important that the children still have interesting choices that are different from day to day—not just crayons to scribble with every afternoon. Plan for variety.

- **Novelty helps.** Bring out materials that may not have been available earlier in the day.

- **Have a grooming time.** At the end of the day, as pick-up time approaches, take time to clean up the children in preparation to go home. Turn this into a self-image enhancer. Bring out a special mirror and a stack of damp facecloths. Bring children to the "magic mirror" one at a time. Let the child wipe his own face with the damp washcloth, and then you can help a little bit. Brush his hair. Admire the child. Talk about his eyes, hair, and so on. When you are finished, comment on what a good-looking group of children they are and how nice everybody looks now that they are all cleaned up.

- **Give special attention.** The part of the day when all except one or two children have gone home can feel a little sad. Use this time to make these children feel special. Perhaps there's a toy a child loves that is in high demand. Bring it out now when he doesn't have to compete for it. Or save a special book for this time or give some extra cuddle time in the rocking chair.

- **Offer "clean," soothing activities.** Some good ones follow below.

TRANSITION ACTIVITY

Zipper-Closure Bag Painting

Materials
zipper-closure plastic bags
2 colors of tempera paint or fingerpaint

To Do
Let the child choose two colors of paint. Put a spoonful of each into the bag and zip it closed. The child can then spread the paint around inside the bag, "draw" on the paint bag with a fingertip, and so on.

Bags of Shaving Cream

Materials

plastic zipper-closure bags
shaving cream
food coloring

To Do

Squeeze shaving cream into the bag. Let the child pick two colors of food coloring. Put a squirt of each into the bag with the shaving cream, on opposite sides of the bag. Zip the bag closed and let the child squeeze it to mix the colors. This is very soothing.

Our Day Story

To Do

Tell a simple story in "Once upon a time" format about what happened that day. "*Once upon a time, there was a great group of kids called the Bumble Bees. They arrived at Miss Suzie's room in the morning, and guess what she had out for them to play with? Playdough! When they finished playing with playdough they went outside and Miss Suzie pushed Max on the swing. Then Molly rode the horsie around the circle…*" Go through all your routines, including what you ate for lunch, nap time, and so on. See how closely they listen and if they beam with pride when they hear their own name in the story.

This late-day activity gives children a verbal review of what they did, and ends the day in a positive way.

Reunions With Parents

High drama here! Reunions are emotionally charged. At this time of day, parents are often in a hurry or have just been battling rush-hour traffic and are tense. Here are some things you can do to help:

- **Encourage the parent to be as consistent as possible with pick-up time.** (This is not to say the parent should never pick up the child early.) When the child notices that the parent comes every day right after story time, for instance, he is more prepared and can relax.

- **Gather each child's things in one place.** This is helpful to parents because they won't have to go looking for socks, jackets, and so on.

- **Locate the child's security item.** Be sure to have the child's stuffed animal or blanket in the cubby, ready to go home.

- **Assemble all of the parent communications.** Programs have various means of daily written communication with parents, such as "What We Did Today" notes, communications on diapering and eating, or notebooks that are passed between the childcare center and home. Make sure these are completed and ready for the parents to take home.

- **Let parents know what went on.** Digital or instant photos are wonderful to show the parents, either individually or on a parent bulletin board, what went on that day.

- **Be accessible to talk to parents.** Have activities that are simple to supervise set up for the children (see pages 127-128) so that you can talk to the parents, but still keep one eye on the children. If you are the only staff person left in the room, reading stories is not such a good idea because children will become distracted when you stop reading to talk to parents.

- **Greet the person who picks up the child warmly, by name.** It is a nice stress reducer. Of course, if you don't know the person, check the person's picture identification and make sure he or she is listed in the child's file as someone who can pick up the child.

- **Have something positive to tell the parent about the child's day**—a cute thing the child said or did, an activity he enjoyed, and so on. This tells parents that you enjoy taking care of their child.

- **Notice the fireworks.** Help the parent notice the expression of joy on the child's face when they reunite. Reconfirm for the parent that he or she is Number One with that child. *"We had a good time and played many different things today, but look at the joy when you come in the room! I can tell you are very special to him."* The parent really needs to hear this. You could even make a collection of joyous reunion photos.

TRANSITION ACTIVITY
Parent/Child Reunion Reading

If the parent and child picked out a book in the morning (see page 64), now is the time to take a few minutes and read it. Have a nice, cozy place set up where they can settle down to enjoy the book together. Then ask them to put it back in the special basket.

When the Child Acts Out at Reunion Time

While joyous reunions are the norm, it is not uncommon for toddlers to cry or run away when the parent walks through the door. This is embarrassing to the parent who may think that the child doesn't love him or her as much as the caregiver, or prefers the childcare center to home. The parent really needs your reassurance at this time. Explain that the child cries to release tension when his most beloved shows up. He feels safe. Reassure parents that crying in this way is common for young children. You might also remind parents that this is the same child who cried at parting from them in the morning. This type of "reunion crying" usually happens only when the child is relatively new to a childcare program.

Another interesting thing happens when the parent shows up—parent and caregiver enter the "no-man's-land" of responsibility. Children often take this time to take advantage of the adults' ambiguity. The caregiver may hesitate to correct the child or handle a situation because the parent is there. And the parent, believing she or he is on the caregiver's turf, may also hesitate to intervene. What opportunistic toddler wouldn't take advantage of this situation? It's a good idea to talk to the parent about this ahead of time, and then just handle the situation with good humor.

A favorite trick of toddlers is to run away from the parent, playing hard to get, often to the annoyance of the parent. It seems that the more rushed the parent is, the more the child wants to do this. It is probably a way that the child has invented to reconnect to the parent. Help out in this situation. Catch the child and say, *"You think you can run away, but we can catch you."* If the child screams in protest, just give a quick hug and say, *"I know, we have lots of fun here, but it's time to go home where there will be fun too! We'll see you tomorrow!*

Goodbye Song

To Do

As a child leaves, encourage the other children to wave goodbye and sing this song to the tune of "He's Got the Whole World in His Hands."

> *Good-bye, Max,*
> *See you tomorrow (or another day, Monday).*
> *Good-bye, Max,*
> *See you tomorrow.*
> *Good-bye Max, see you tomorrow.*
> *Then we can play some more.*

The departing child, of course, can wave goodbye too. This strengthens bonds of friendship between the children.

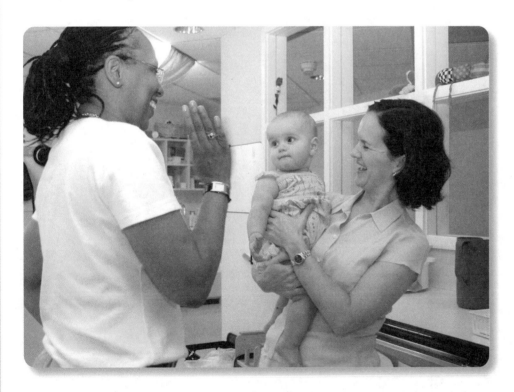

Congratulations! You made it to the end of the day! Take a moment for reflection. Think about what went well today (always start with the positive). Get your room in order. Think about what will happen the next day and rearrange anything or have materials ready to set out in the morning. Write any necessary notes to the person who opens in the morning.

Now, consider your own transition back to "civilian life." One teacher says she opens her car windows and plays loud rock music all the way home, just to release tension and relax. Someone else might sit quietly with a cup of tea. A short walk in nature is another caregiver's end-of-day ritual. Someone else loves a bubble bath. Create your own transition ritual…and go home and enjoy the next piece of your day, knowing that you have created a good experience for the children in your care.

Staff Training for Successful Transitions

Whether you are orienting new staff, revisiting a topic with experienced caregivers, or presenting a workshop, stepping away and looking at the topics you are going to staff on in a more abstract way help people to gain insights.

Personalize

With any topic, it's a good idea to start with the personal experiences and feelings of the person or people being trained. Have people examine how they feel about transitions in general. Invite them to name some transitions they have experienced, such as moving to a new school, going from middle school to high school, starting college, getting married, having kids, starting a new job, losing a parent, and so on. How did they feel? What things helped? What would have made it easier? They are likely to list such things as rehearsals, knowing what to expect, having someone there to depend on, and knowing what was expected of them. You can then help them translate these ideas to the infants and toddlers in their care. How can they make a child feel safe? How can they give the child "rehearsals?" Who can the child depend on? How will the child know what is expected?

Nonverbal Communication

Do you know two people who speak a language not understood by those being trained? Ask them to talk to each other in their language, pretending that they are afraid, angry, tired, happy, loving, and so on. Can the observers tell what is going on, which emotions are being expressed? (You could also simply ask people to act out these emotions using "gibberish" or even charades.) Then ask people how they knew what emotions were being expressed. Facial expressions? Gestures? Tone of voice?

Invite people to think about their pets. Dogs especially know ahead of time when the master is going out, about to eat, leaving on a trip, and so on. How do they know this? Repeated actions, certain smells, clothing signals, the appearance of a suitcase, and so on are all clues for the pet. Point out that infants and toddlers learn these signals as well.

Invite people to list other nonverbal cues for actions that are present in their own lives: alarm clocks, stoplights, and the smell of lunch being cooked. Again, help them translate this concept to their classrooms. How do children know what's going to happen? Ask participants to think of and list other nonverbal signals they can introduce into the routines of their day.

Feeding Infants

For an interesting exercise, ask pairs of people to feed each other applesauce or pudding. While in the role of the infant, one becomes more conscious of the importance of giving the child enough time to swallow, and of recognizing when the child is ready for another spoonful.

Also discuss how to deal with infants who are hungry and are waiting to be fed while the caregiver is busy with another child. Use the example described on pages 40-41 about how it feels to be ignored by a waitress in a restaurant. Have people describe other incidents in their lives when they were ignored while trying to get someone's attention and describe the emotions they felt at the time. Conclude by encouraging people to acknowledge the waiting infants and talk to them.

Rituals

Encourage staff to think about what a ritual is and rituals they perform in their own lives. It could be the order of the service in their church, singing the national anthem before sports events, what they do before going to bed at night, how they make their coffee, and so on. Discuss the use of rituals, and ask why we follow them. They make people feel comfortable and give them a sense of belonging. They help people remember things.

Ask them to describe and list the rituals they already have in place in the routine of their day with children. Then think about and discuss other rituals they could build in to their day, and what purpose the rituals would serve.

Late-Afternoon or Bad-Weather Fun

Discuss why it is so important that the late afternoon is as much a quality time for children as other times of the day. Analyze why it can be difficult and brainstorm solutions. Ask each participant to bring to the meeting at least one activity he or she likes to do in the late afternoon. It could be set up as a participation workshop.

Assemble a "Late Afternoon Fun Box" for each classroom, similar to the Bad-Weather Fun Box described on page 126. Teachers could play one of the children's favorite music cassettes or CDs or read something special, such as "touch and feel" books. Perhaps you could bring out a bunch of small stuffed animals, such as Beanie Babies®, to play with the children. Colorful, gauzy scarves are fun to play with. Just be sure to put these things back in the decorated "Late Afternoon Fun Box" and put them away again at the end of the afternoon. Keep them special for that time of day.

The Problem Hat Game

This is a "What Would You Do If…?" game. On separate slips of paper, at least one for each participant, describe a problem or a difficult situation involving a transition. Fold the slips of paper and put them in a hat. One at a time, each participant pulls a piece of paper out of the hat, reads it out loud, and then describes how he or she would handle the situation. Encourage discussion and emphasize that there may be more than one acceptable solution.

Learn Transition Songs

As a group, learn the songs in this book for the various transitions described. Sing them together. Discuss why songs are effective transition aids. Make up your own songs, or substitute songs you already know and like. Add songs for transitions not covered in this book.

SIMPLE TRANSITIONS FOR INFANTS AND TODDLERS

Appendix

Developmental Notes

How to Set Up a Positive Learning Environment

Setting Up the Outdoor Environment

Recommended Books

Developmental Notes

Welcome to the most dynamic period of growth and learning in the human life span. Children between the ages of birth and three are making almost daily changes. Infants and toddlers are constantly evolving. For the purposes of this book an infant is from birth to 18 months of age. The age range of a toddler, one who is up and "toddling," is anywhere from 13 months to 3 years of age. Yes, there is an overlap. This is to allow for individual differences in maturation.

There are certain behaviors that we can expect from children at various ages in their development. Taking these normal behaviors into account as we care for children can guide us in teaching them. Instead of fighting nature, we can use the children's interests and capabilities to make them feel secure and cooperative.

Children must first feel safe in order to benefit from your program.
If a child is tense and fearful, little learning will be possible. The child must feel safe and relaxed to explore the environment and benefit from all the possibilities offered. But how do you make an infant or toddler feel safe? Although you can talk to them and reassure them, words alone do not comfort them.

Therefore: Give children familiar adults they can depend on. Primary caregivers can make the child feel loved and secure. Caregivers should be responsive to the infant, letting the child know he has communicated effectively. In addition, the environment and the flow of the day should be predictable.

Infants and toddlers become attached to a limited number of people.
Helpless infants need adults to care for and protect them. At first, newborns attach to just one or two people, those who take on the parenting role. Gradually, infants can add others to a small circle of people to whom they are attached. In child care, when an infant (and a toddler is still an infant) has a firm attachment to one caregiver, the child feels safe enough to relax, play, try new things, and be generally cooperative. When there are too many caregivers, the child may feel overwhelmed and shut down emotionally or act out continuously.

Therefore: Facilitate an attachment to a particular "primary caregiver." This is the caregiver who should greet the child in the morning (if possible), comfort, feed, and diaper the child and do the main communicating with the parents. Also, do your best to arrange your staffing to limit the number of adults who care for the child. If the caregiver to whom the child is attached is present, then the child can accept other adults in the environment. Gradually, the child will become comfortable with several familiar adults.

Very young children like things to be predictable. Because they don't understand much language, their feelings of security come from knowing what is going to happen next, how things are done, and so on. This may be one reason a toddler likes you to read the same book or sing the same songs over and over again. It gives them a feeling of control when they know what is on the next page.

Therefore: Keep the framework of your day basically the same from day to day, and have plenty of familiar objects around, such as favorite books and toys. Repeat many of their favorite activities and songs often. Weave new activities into the context of the familiar.

It is difficult for infants and toddlers to separate from parents or people to whom they are attached. Learning to separate from loved ones is actually a life-long learning process, and for many people it is never easy. We have to acknowledge that infants and toddlers have these powerful feelings, and we must allow these feelings. What makes it difficult is that we cannot comfort young children with words, and they have no concept of time. Temperament also plays a part in how children handle separation. Some children even experience distress when their caregiver leaves the room for a few minutes.

Therefore: Be patient. Do not try to hurry the child out of separation distress. Let children express themselves with their cries, while you hold and comfort them. The one thing that helps is consistency of experience. Over time, the child will realize that the parent comes back and that he will not be harmed while the parent is away. It helps if the same caregiver receives the child each day, and the parent is consistent in the time of pick up.

Toddlers struggle for independence. As children advance toward and through the toddler years, they develop an increasing urge to resist adults and do things for themselves. They want to find their own way in the world. They are learning about where their personal power starts and ends.

Therefore: Don't require that they follow you in lock-step order. Give children several choices of acceptable responses when you can, and let them think that a particular action was their own idea. Also make it possible for them to do as much as possible for themselves, even if it takes more time.

Infants and toddlers are very involved with objects. Objects frame the world for infants and toddlers. Objects are concrete – things you can see and touch. Infants and toddlers want to explore every object that comes their way. The objects present in any situation help children understand what's going to happen. They "read" objects before they understand words. A blanket may mean it's time to rest. Plates on the table mean lunch. Coats mean outside time.

Therefore: Try to find objects that represent various parts of your routine. When the children see them, they know what is going to happen and are more likely to cooperate on their own, without so much cajoling from you.

Transitional objects help them through difficulties. A stuffed animal, a blanket, or some other "lovey" is a very special object that the child has adopted to represent "home," "mommy," "love," "security," and so on. Often, these objects are not something the adults in their lives suggest, but rather, something the child invents. Sometimes called "security objects," these objects seem to carry a little magic inside and help the child calm down and gain the courage to face the wider world. They can be very helpful in comforting children who are crying at separation or when they are hurt, and in settling them down to sleep. Most children are very possessive about their transitional objects and don't want other children playing with them. This is one thing they should not be required to share. Useful as they are, sometimes these special objects become cumbersome or can interfere in other play or learning situations.

Therefore: Create a special place where children can place their "loveys" and still have access to them whenever they need them. Cubbies often work for this purpose. They can be brought out routinely at rest time. But you can encourage children to put them away in their cubbies themselves at other times of the day, such as when they are doing messy activities or going outside.

Young children are intrigued by novelty. Children are attracted to the "new thing," but only if they are surrounded with the familiar. If everything is new, anxiety builds and the child can seem overwhelmed, such as when the child first enters childcare. However, if a new toy appears, everybody wants to play with it, although its play value may be less than familiar objects. The children are curious. They want to find out about the new object.

Therefore: Use their interest in something novel when you want to get their attention or gather them together. An object can be used to introduce a new book, for instance. Pulling an object out of a "Treasure Box," as described on page 97 can be an effective way to entice a group of toddlers to gather together.

Children under the age of three have only a limited understanding of time. Infants and toddlers live in the here and now. They can only keep in mind what is in front of their faces. They think very little of the future. Words like "soon" are very relative in meaning. When a caregiver tries to comfort a grieving toddler by saying, "Mommy will be back soon," it is not consoling or helpful to an infant or toddler. While toddlers don't have enough experience to know what a minute or an hour is, or what yesterday and tomorrow mean, they do learn to tell time by the sequence of events and the routines of the day.

Therefore: Try to do certain segments of your routine in the same order every day. It's okay to use time words such as "minute" or "hour" in your speech because children learn the meaning of these words by hearing them used in context over a long period of time; but don't expect infants and toddlers to understand their meaning. Encourage parents, as much as possible, to arrive to pick up the child at the same time every day.

Infants and toddlers usually don't stay with an activity for long periods of time. Generally speaking, infants and toddlers don't spend very long doing one particular thing. They flit from toy to toy and activity to activity. (The exception is when the child is working on a new, emerging skill. Then the child can keep at it for an amazing amount of time.)

Therefore: Have a variety of simple toys and activities available and organize so you or the children can put the toys away easily. When you offer special activities, such as art, make it something quick and easy. Don't be discouraged if the child fingerpaints for three minutes and then wants to do something else.

Young children are easily distracted. One reason toddlers flit from activity to activity is that they are easily distracted. They are playing with something, hear an interesting noise or see something else appealing, and the toy they were playing with is dropped. They are off to the new thing.

Therefore: Low dividers in a room can create a visual barrier that helps reduce distractions. Various play areas and nooks and crannies help children concentrate. It's not wise to do music with some of the children when you want others to play independently.

Young children are influenced by what others are doing. Because they are easily distracted, what another child is doing looks very interesting. A toy that someone else is playing with looks more interesting than that same toy sitting on the shelf. A child looking at a book glances up and sees two children crawling through a tunnel. That looks like fun. The book is dropped and the child goes over to join the other children in that activity. It can be a problem when so many children start doing something that it creates crowding and pushing.

Therefore: When you want children to join the others, start doing something with the children near you. It will look interesting and the others will be drawn over to you. When you see that a space is getting too crowded and there is pushing and an accident is likely to happen or tempers are likely to flare, start something else in a different area of the room. That will draw off some of the children. This is easiest to do if there are several adults in the room to divert the attention.

Imitation is a major play and learning mode for infants and toddlers. Both infants and toddlers like to do what other children around them are doing. They don't need any coaching for this. Very young infants just gaze into the faces of other children. Soon they start imitating gestures and sounds. Toddlers mimic everything their friends do. This is one of the first ways they establish friendships.

Therefore: Position infants near each other. Give toddlers duplicate or similar toys to play with side by side. Capitalize on this by teaching them fingerplays, simple songs, and movement games.

Toddlers love repetition. It is not surprising that "again" is an early vocabulary word for toddlers. They love having you read the same picture book several times. They like to sing the same song over again. Familiar art projects, sensory activities, and play materials get eager participation.

Therefore: This makes it easier for you to have a solid, stable daily order of routines. Also, don't feel you have to come up with something new every day. Develop a collection of "old stand-bys" that you know children enjoy. Add variety in small steps, such as changing the color of the playdough or adding a new object to use when playing with it. Start and end with a familiar story and read a new book in between.

Children like to play with adults. There is nothing more interesting than an adult on the floor. When you are on their level, infants and toddlers love to come over to you, drape themselves on you, and snuggle in close.

Therefore: When you want children to come over to you and do something, simply get down on the floor and start doing it with one or two of them.

They don't plan ahead. Unlike a four- or five-year-old who may be thinking ahead about the block structure he plans to build or the action game he will play with his friends, a toddler doesn't think about future play activities. He is influenced by what he sees right now.

Therefore: Put the things you want the child to play with in his line of vision. If the child comes in and there is playdough on the table, he is more likely to be attracted to it, than to go looking for something. If you want to encourage sand play outside, place some attractive objects and toys in the sandbox ahead of time.

Young children are egocentric. Very young children cannot see things from someone else's point of view. They don't have enough experience for that. Other children are seen as accessories to the environment that are put there for this child's pleasure. If a child wants a toy someone else is playing with, she thinks that everyone wants her to have that toy, so she takes it and is genuinely surprised and intrigued by the protest at the other end of the toy. Sharing and taking turns are not natural tendencies for this age.

Therefore: It takes a lot of gentle coaching to teach the child to be considerate of others and learn the give and take of play. Model the process yourself. Help children state their wishes and be heard by their playmates. It is one of the major social learnings of the toddler years. There will be endless opportunities!

"Meltdowns" are common with toddlers. Because they are so egocentric and inexperienced in give and take, toddlers sometimes lose control and have tantrums. They are frustrated that they cannot have what they want, and they may be frustrated that they cannot express themselves. They are also testing the extent of their personal power. What can they get others to do?

Therefore: Try not to get angry or embarrassed when a child has a tantrum. It is not a reflection on you. Stay calm. Do not let the child "succeed" by getting what he wants. Be sympathetic, yet firm. If the child cannot calm down, remove him from the other children to a different part of the room. Your "cozy corner" is a good choice (see page 123). Don't give a lot of attention to the screaming child, other than general supervision so that he doesn't hurt himself. Let the child know he can come back and join you whenever he wants to, when he has calmed down. Sometimes offering the child a glass of water helps to stop the tantrum.

Developing Language Skills

Infants and toddlers understand a lot, almost from the very beginning, and their understanding grows as their vocabulary develops. There are three major ideas to understand when we think about the role of language in gaining children's cooperation during transition times. 1) There is more to language than words. 2) Understanding comes before speaking. 3) You are modeling language for them. They learn to talk by hearing you.

Understanding the Nonverbal Aspects of Language

Gestures, intonations, and tone of voice make up a big piece of meaning. Just try taking these elements out of your adult speech. It's hard to do! The lack of these things makes it harder for the listener to discern your meaning. These are the first elements of speech we learn, and babies "understand" them almost from the beginning.

Gestures and Body Language

Infants and toddlers understand body language. Hold your hands out to an infant sitting on the floor or one who is being held, and they will most likely lean toward you and hold their hands out to reach for you (as long as they know you and feel safe). A very young baby learns this quickly. Even when they cannot yet hold out their hands in response, you can see their body get ready to be picked up. There are many other examples of body language that a child learns to understand. Hold your hand out, palm up, and the child likely will put something in your hand. The child discerns your interest when you sit down next to her or when you lean forward toward her. Nodding and shaking one's head to mean yes and no are other examples. A shrug of the shoulder means indifference. Raised shoulders and arms bent at the elbow, hands out can indicate frustration or giving up.

Gestures are specific hand and arm movements that have an intended meaning. They vary in different cultures. Waving "bye-bye" is one of the first gestures a young child learns. There are many others such as: motioning someone to come closer, or patting the floor near you; waggling your finger as a warning not to do somethino; clapping hands to denote approval; a mock wipe of the brow to indicate relief. How young children love to point at things to say, "Hey....look at that!"

Tone of Voice

Tone of voice is how we communicate the emotion connected with what we are saying. This piece of language is universal. Human beings all over the world can understand each other at this basic level. You could be dropped at any remote place on the planet and just by listening to people, even those you cannot see, know if they are afraid, rored, stressed, angry, gleeful, or even in love. Infants seem to be programmed to understand this piece of language from the beginning. A calm, loving voice helps settle them down and make them feel secure. Shouting and anger in the environment causes them to tense up. And we all know, crying causes them to cry!

So, realize that whatever you say to them, your tone of voice is most important. You can say the same words in a playful, friendly way, or an angrq, forceful way. They are much more likely to relax and be inclifed to do whatever you want them to do if your voice is light and easy. Toddlers have lots of "accidents" – spills, knocking things over, toileting accidents, and so on. Your tone of voice in dealing with these situations—light and easy or angry and frustrated—can make the difference in how the child feels. This is even more important with toddlers than with older children who understand your words, because toddlers get the whole meaning from your nonverbal language.

Intonation

Intonation is the melody of your sentences—how your voice rises and falls within a phrase. Although we share many basic intonations, there is some variation between languages and cultures here. A question usually rises at the end of the phrase. A command usually has a falling intonation at the end.

This is another aspect of language infants and toddlers learn very early. We've been taught that when we address older children, never to phrase a request as a question. When we need children to put toys away, for example, we know not to use a speech convention that we use when we're being polite to adults and say, "Do you want to clean up now?" because they'll take you seriously and feel they have an option in their response. Instead, we say, "It's time to clean up now." Likewise, when we talk to infants and toddlers, we need our intonations to say what we really mean.

Eye Contact

When you make eye contact with anyone it is a connecting thing. It says, "My brain is talking to your brain." When eye contact does not happen, there is no stirring within. That is why it is more difficult to make eye contact with someone when we have something difficult or upsetting to say. Eye contact intensifies emotion.

It is interesting that children don't learn "gaze aversion" until late in toddlerhood. As adults, unless we are in love with the person in front of us, we rarely stare into another adult's eyes for more than a few seconds. Something makes us move our eyes away for an instant at least. It is too close, too unnerving. Infants and toddlers, on the other hand, use their steady eye contact to "capture" us, and we are very vulnerable. We fall in love with them! We take care of them.

It is quite important to make good eye contact with infants and toddlers when we speak to them and want them to do something. It tells them, I am talking to you. I want you to connect with me.

Facial Expressions

All over the world, people have the same facial expressions to express basic emotions. Infants learn quickly to understand facial expressions. If your face registers alarm from across the room, an infant or toddler will stop what they are doing…at least momentarily. Where you can make great use of facial expression is when you first greet the child in the morning. Brighten your eyes and soften your face with a big smile of delight and the child will understand, *I am welcome here.*

Understanding Comes Before Speaking

Young children are surrounded by speech. They hear the spoken word from day one. When certain words accompany a repeated action or are said when the child sees an object repeatedly over a period of time, the child begins to understand specific words. Examples: "Up!"; "Cup;" "All gone;" "Uh-oh!" They already understand all of the non-verbal things described above. Now they associate certain sounds with meanings as well. This happens well before a child is one year old.

When you work with infants and toddlers talk a lot and surround the child with meaningful language, so that this understood vocabulary will increase over time.

Model Concrete Language

Because of their limited life experience, very young children best understand language that describes the here and now – what is in front of their faces. They need to be able to see and touch something, or otherwise experience it with their senses to understand the words that describe them. You can greatly enhance their language learning simply by describing what the children are seeing and doing. *"This playdough is warm. See how soft it feels? I'll give some red playdough to Molly and some blue playdough to Max."*

Nouns (people and things) are among the first words of toddlers, such as *"Ba-ba (bottle)," "kitty,"* and *"Dada." "Mine!"* is a word that follows quickly afterwards, especially with children who are cared for in groups. In addition, social words and gestures are some of the first to emerge in young toddlers, for example, *"Hi"* and *"Bye-bye," "Night-night"*…daily routines!

"Telegraphic speech" is the common mode of toddlers. One word holds a world of meaning for them. "Cookie!" It is the job of adults to embroider the single word utterances, giving the children models of other words they can combine with them. *"Oh – you're hungry. You want to eat a cookie. Here is a cookie for you."*

Also take every opportunity to describe emotions. "You made her happy when you let her play with you. See her face? She is smiling." "Max is sad because he misses his mommy. See…he is crying." If we can help these youngest people learn to recognize and name their emotions early in their lives, we will have given them a valuable gift.

Learn to Speak "Motherese"

While most people who work with toddlers do this naturally, it bears mentioning. Psychologists have coined the term motherese or parentese for the way that skillful parents automatically speak to their very young children. Many mothers seem to know instinctively how to provide just the right delivery and challenge in their language when they speak to their child. Their voice typically goes up, just a little bit, the pace of their language slows down, and their speech is simplified. They tend to talk to the child "one step up" from where the child is in his verbal abilities, just a little more complex. The language is clear and descriptive. Sentences become more complex as the child progresses.

You have a group of children, not just one. They will be at different levels of development and their verbal skills will vary. Make sure you really talk to individual children. Then, as you address one child in front of you, you will probably adjust your language to what you know the child can handle. The better you know the children in your care, the more effectively you will be able to communicate.

Infants and toddlers are truly "in transition." Their development is speeding along and you can almost notice daily changes. That is what makes working with this age so exciting. You will probably record major milestones of each child's development in their records or portfolio. But be sure to notice the daily, little things as well. Being "in tune" with the children in front of you is the most important thing you can do to make your day go smoothly.

How to Set Up a Positive Learning Environment

Infants, toddlers, and two-year-olds live a large portion of their lives in the indoor and outdoor space you set up for them. This environment should allow a wide range of physical activity and be attractive for children and adults alike. How you divide, organize, and equip your indoor and outdoor space influences the effectiveness of your program. It also is an outward reflection of your philosophy. It tells people what you value and how you feel about children. The people and the atmosphere you create in your interactions with children and their parents is the most important aspect of your program, but your physical environment is a critical tool for creating quality care for infants and toddlers. It can work with you or against you.

The Play Area

If children are not sleeping, eating, or being diapered, they should be in the play area. This is a place for free exploration and movement where a child can experiment with objects and practice emerging motor skills. For this reason, this space must be absolutely safe for babies.

When deciding what equipment to put in the play area, think about all the things that infants and toddlers enjoy doing—rolling, crawling, going up stairs, pulling up, cruising, climbing, banging things together, throwing things, dumping containers, and poking things into holes. Consciously arrange your environment so children can practice these and other new and emerging skills in as many ways as possible.

Nooks and Crannies

Create nooks and crannies for children to crawl into, but not so small that they get stuck. When young children explore such spaces they are learning about their bodies in space, such as how big they are and where they fit. They also use these places as "peek-a-boo" centers, making the world disappear and reappear when they crawl in and out. These spaces can be very simple, such as a blanket thrown over a low, sturdy table or some cardboard boxes from the grocery store.

Different Levels

Crawling babies and new walkers also like to explore different levels and surfaces. Ramps, low platforms to climb up and down from, couch cushions placed on the floor, and plastic wading pools filled with various things like soft balls or small stuffed animals are all possibilities.

Adult Furniture

Adults should be comfortable too. A loveseat, soft chair, or small couch makes a good place to settle down with a child to cuddle, enjoy a book, or play.

Baby Traps

If your program has a wind-up swing, walker, infant seat, or bouncing chair, use it sparingly. Children cannot explore or use their muscles freely when they are confined in these devices. The only reason to have them in the environment is to keep children safe when the adult is otherwise occupied in the room.

Tips for Organizing the Play Area

- You may want to dedicate one part of your play area for "tummy babies"—the not yet crawling or toddling infants. This is to protect them from older children who may accidentally step on them, fall over them, or poke and bother them.

- You can use manufactured dividers, bolsters, or pillows to accomplish this. If you don't have such a divided area, be sure to stay close to a non-mobile baby.

- Put a clean blanket on the floor for tummy babies to lie on, or place a clean sheet over an area rug and tuck it under the edges. This can be washed at the end of the day.

- In the crawler-cruiser area for the older infants, have a sturdy toy shelf for toys. It should be very stable, in case a child decides to pull up on it.

- Try to place toys in the same place every day so that children know where to find them. You could "label" places for toys with either photographs or a picture of each toy cut from old catalogs and placed on the shelf covered with clear contact paper. This creates a matching game for older toddlers. Of course, children will carry toys all over the place and will not necessarily be able to put them back in the right place. At least this will help keep you organized.

- Collect interesting containers. Infants and toddlers are often as fascinated by the container as by the toy itself. One way to add new life to your room is simple to change the containers that things are in. Plastic tote bins are great. Consider also plastic dish tubs, plastic baskets, trays, shoeboxes, shopping bags, shoe bags, cardboard boxes, and laundry baskets.

- Create "mini-environments" inside your shelves by covering pieces of cardboard that just fit inside the back wall spaces with various fabrics, pictures, or Plexiglas mirrors.

- Place photographs of children and families and interesting pictures cut from magazines at the children's eye level. These can be laminated or covered with clear contact paper. Do not use staples or thumbtacks.

- Store toys that are currently not in use. If you rotate toys, putting some away and bringing them out again after a few months, they will seem totally new to the children. Keep favorite toys available all the time, though, especially if a child seems to particularly enjoy and look for a certain toy.

Expanding the Play Area for Active Toddlers

More distinct areas of your play environment can be developed as children grow. When toddlers see a large, open space they want to run, so it's a good idea to divide play space with low dividers such as toy shelves. Because toddlers are easily distracted by other children, they may play with greater concentration if they are out of the direct line of sight of their playmates.

Messy Play

When not in use for food service, low tables can be used for messy activities such as art, playdough, and clay. Place the tables over a hard floor for easy cleanup. Hang waterproof smocks nearby, for your own convenience. A sensory table could be here, as well.

A Climber

Because toddlers are compulsive climbers, have available a stable climber designed for this age group, with a padded mat underneath it. Other good additions are a collapsible tunnel, riding toys, and a rocking boat.

Dramatic Play

A simple dramatic play setting can be set apart from the rest of the play area, making it a special space. A room divider could provide one wall. A window made from a picture or travel poster and curtains is another idea. Enrich dramatic play with dolls, cooking utensils, a telephone, dress-up clothes, and a mirror.

Books

No program for children is complete without a good assortment of quality children's literature. While you may keep some books out of reach and bring them out only when you are able to supervise closely, you should make other books accessible to infants and toddlers. A low bookshelf, good lighting, and a cozy chair, as well as some stuffed animals to read to, make this area inviting.

Toys and Blocks

Sturdy, low toy shelves can hold simple puzzles, large pegs and pegboards, shape boxes, pounding benches, stacking cups and rings, push toys, pull toys, toy vehicles, and a wide assortment of homemade toys. A laundry basket could hold a variety of balls. Large, lightweight blocks are best for this age group. Toddlers feel powerful when the lift something big. They love to knock down a tower of blocks, so use blocks made of cardboard or vinyl-covered foam. Wooden unit blocks can be introduced as children approach age three.

The Parent Area

Of course, parents of enrolled children have access to your whole environment, but make sure parents feel comfortable and communication is easy.

Communicating with parents can be a challenge with several staff people working different shifts and busy parents coming and going at different hours. You might consider creating a special area near the entrance of your room. In this area, there should also be a place or cubby labeled for each child's belongings. Many programs label each child's cubby with the child's photo and name. Things you might have in the parent area:

- A bench or other comfortable place to sit down while removing children's outer clothing—a place to cuddle and say goodbye. This should be near the children's cubbies.

- A bulletin board with items of general interest for parents, such as notices of special events, interesting articles, photos of the children playing, descriptions of things children did or said, and announcements of births or news of other families.

- Photos of other families whose children are in the program, to encourage parents to get to know each other.

- A parent-lending library specific to the needs of infants and toddlers.

- A lost-and-found spot. Encourage parents to label everything with the child's name. Have a fabric-marking pen available for parents to use to label the child's clothing, and tape and a marking pen for other belongings.

(Adapted from **Simple Steps** by Karen Miller, published by Gryphon House, Inc., 1999 (pp. 229-237). Reprinted with permission.)

Setting Up the Outdoor Environment

Most programs that serve both infants and toddlers provide one play space that they must share. This can be done with good planning and supervision. Just as with play spaces for older children, an infant/toddler play yard can be designed with zones to facilitate play and supervision. You could have a grassy, shaded section for small babies. In another zone could be a small climber and swings, and in a third area, space for riding toys, sand play, and water play.

Textures and Sensory Delights

Create Interesting Patterns of Light

Trees already create interesting shadows as the leaves move in the breeze. You could also add to the shadow patterns. Out of reach of the children, hang colored pieces of Plexiglas or a crystal to make rainbows to cast interesting colored light onto the playground. You could also attach panels of colored Plexiglas to permanent structures or to a chain link fence. Crawling babies could look through it and see the world change color. Consider hanging large pieces of bright fabrics for the light to shine through. These could also be used as temporary shade structures. It is especially important to have some shade on an infant/toddler playground. If natural shade is not available, canopies could be built on the playground.

Textures

Think about how to add to the interesting textures of your playground. Take a survey of the textures that are already there, accessible to the children. How many do you have? Grass, concrete, sand, chain link? What can you add? A tree stump with bark and tree rings will be interesting for little fingers to explore. Large, smooth rocks, rubber tires, blankets, a small wooden deck, artificial turf, and indoor/outdoor carpeting are all possibilities.

Sounds

Wind chimes are made of many different materials and can create a wide variety of sounds. A windsock with streamers is something beautiful to look at, as well as providing rustling sounds in the breeze. Plastic streamers, such as those used at car dealerships, provide great sounds.

Smells

Flowers can stimulate the sense of smell, but at ground level they will probably not survive the inquisitive hands of investigating explorers. Perhaps you could use window boxes, and then lift the children to smell the flowers. Dandelions, a free and lovely gift of nature, delight babies.

Gross Motor Play

Gross motor activity dominates the play of infants and toddlers. They are very busy learning the mechanics of their bodies and developing strength and coordination. Here are some suggestions to encourage gross motor play:
- Offer tummy time. "Tummy babies," who are not yet crawling or otherwise getting around, can still enjoy the outdoors.
- Crawl: Babies who are crawling or creeping will enjoy moving over textured materials. Make a "texture path" by providing a succession of different textures.
- Cruise.
- Climb.
- Use wheel toys.
- Use balls for kicking, tossing, and catching.

Fine Motor Play

Dumping and Filling

Small wagons and push baskets are popular with toddlers; they combine gross motor and fine motor play.

Sand Play

Sand play gives toddlers on-going opportunities to dump and fill, and they enjoy it for its sensory pleasure, as well. Sand play requires good supervision on the part of teachers, but is definitely worth it. Simply sit with the children and play with the sand next to them, modeling different things to do with sand. If you do this, the children are much less likely to eat and throw the sand, because they will see other interesting things to do with it.

Water Play

Water play in warm weather is endlessly interesting to toddlers and even infants. A dishpan of water placed on the ground near crawling babies will encourage exploration and interest. You could provide water to feel and splash and, at a later time, add interesting things, such as a sponge, boats, and other water toys. **Safety Note:** Even small amounts of water can be dangerous for young children. Supervise closely.

Special Health and Safety Considerations

Remember that even the best-designed playground needs regular maintenance and attention. With infants and toddlers you need to be especially aware of a few things:

- **Ingestible items:** Remember that infants and toddlers put everything in their mouths and sometimes in their noses and ears, as well. Pea gravel and small wood chips are not a good ground surface on an infant/toddler play yard. Look for mushrooms and toadstools, as well as loose debris that the children could choke on. Keep the sandbox covered when it is not in use.

- **Swings:** Older infants and toddlers love swings, but they need close supervision. Toddlers don't "think ahead" and will often walk right in front of a swing. An adult needs to be close by to prevent this. Instead of cute animal figure swings or hard seats, use soft seat, sling-type baby swings.

- **Small spaces and gaps:** Toddlers are attracted to small spaces and have a talent for getting stuck. Make sure that any gaps in climbers and other equipment are more than eight inches so the children will not get their heads stuck. Be sure the fence and gates have no gaps, are not buckled out anywhere, and go all the way down to the ground.

- **Surface irregularities:** New walkers stumble and fall easily. Be conscious of surface irregularities that may present an unnecessary hazard.

- **Wading pools:** Children who are not toilet trained should not use wading pools. You are inviting the spread of infectious diseases, if you put several children in a wading pool. There are many other options for water play that are just as much fun for little ones and much more hygienic.

- **Delicate skin:** Infants and toddlers are even more sensitive than older children to over-exposure to the sun. Do not leave them in the sun for prolonged periods of time without adequate skin protection or clothing cover. Remember that the effects of sunburn do not show up until later.

- **Overheating:** Watch the children closely for signs of overheating. Take them inside or in the shade to cool down and offer liquids. In warm weather, it is very important to give the children plenty of water. A cooler with a spigot and some paper cups on the playground could serve this purpose, if you don't have a drinking fountain.

- **Diapering needs:** Do diapering inside. To prevent the spread of germs, diapers should always be changed at the changing table, rather than on the ground where other children might come along and play.

- **Staff ratios:** Maintain staff ratios outside. Because babies should be on a demand schedule, and often some are sleeping while others are awake and playing, you have to be very flexible. It can work to have one or more teachers stationed outside in nice weather to receive babies who are ready to play. Never leave sleeping babies alone inside. If you have a nice shady area, cribs, baby beds, or buggies can be outside. Consider protecting them with mosquito netting, and, of course, still supervise closely.

(Adapted from ***The Outside Play and Learning Book*** by Karen Miller, published by Gryphon House, Inc., 1989 (pp. 23-26). Reprinted with permission.)

Recommended Books
Books About Separation

Will You Come Back for Me? by Ann Tompert. Illustrated by Robin Kramer. Suki is worried about being left in childcare for the first time. Her mother reassures her that she loves her and will always return for her.

Have You Seen My Duckling? by Nancy Tafuri. One adventurous baby duckling swims away from the others. Mother and the other ducklings travel over the pond asking the inhabitants of the pond, "Have you seen my duckling?"

Where Is Baby's Mommy? by Karen Katz. The baby searches for mommy in this story with easy-to-lift flaps. A delightful interactive book.

Blueberries for Sal by Robert McCloskey. A gentle adventure story that is just right for toddlers. An excellent book for transitioning from baby books to more complex stories.

Good-Bye Daddy! by Bridgette Weinger. Illustrated by Alan Marks. A little boy must say goodbye to his father because they live in different homes. The love and caring shown by the father helps with the separation.

Hello! Good-bye! by Aliki. There are many different kinds of hellos and just as many kinds of goodbyes. Each can be filled with excitement and surprise.

Books About Security Objects

How a Baby Grows by Nola Buck. Illustrated by Pamela Paparone. An active story about the things a growing child sees, needs, speaks, hears, and shares.

Tom and Pippo Read a Story by Helen Oxenbury. Tom exhausts his father by asking him to keep reading books to him. At last, father thinks he is finished, but clever Tom decides that Pippo, his pet monkey, also needs a story.

The Bear Went Over the Mountain by Rosemary Wells. The specific action of the bear is illustrated as he takes his trip over the mountain with his basket. His basket is empty when he starts, but full of flowers when he arrives home.

Golden Bear by Ruth Young. Illustrated by Rachel Isadora. A beautifully illustrated story about a little boy and his perfect companion.

Carl Goes to Day Care by Alexandra Day. Mom drops off the baby and Carl (her dog) at the childcare center. The teacher gets locked outside and Carl takes over. This story encourages children to use their imaginations.

Tom and Pippo by Helen Oxenbury. The first story that Helen Oxenbury wrote when she created Tom and Pippo. It's the story of a young boy and his toy monkey that goes everywhere with him. All of the **Tom and Pippo** books are full of expressions and feelings that are common to young children.

Barney Is Best by Nancy White Carlstrom. Illustrated by James Graham Hale. A trip to the hospital can be scary but it's not bad if you have a special friend along with you.

Books About Friendship

All Fall Down and Clap Hands by Helen Oxenbury. These are two of a four-title series of large-format board books for babies and toddlers. Helen Oxenbury's double-page watercolor illustrations are filled with big, beautiful multi-ethnic babies enjoying the active rhyming text related to the actions the babies are doing.

Tom and Pippo Make a Friend by Helen Oxenbury. Tom and Pippo find themselves playing in a sandbox while making a new friend.

Baby and Friends by Paul Bricknell. This is a title from one of the best, soft padded board-book series, with photographs of babies with their toys and their furry friends, and babies interacting together.

First Friends by Lenore Blegvad. Illustrated by Erik Blegvad. Making new friends is the theme of this delightful story. Toddlers are playing with their toys independently and as the story progresses, children begin to share their toys and play together, without the assistance of an adult.

Friends by Rachel Isadora. Children are busy playing, jumping, and drawing in small groups and alone. These familiar scenes delight children as they listen to the story.

Friends at School by Rochelle Bunett. Photographs by Matt Brown. These full-color photographs tell the story of children with a variety of abilities playing together. This book shares the importance of inclusion for all children.

Moonbeam's Friend by Frank Asch. This board book is a simple story of friendship between Moonbeam (a big bear) and bird, his very small friend.

At Preschool With Teddy Bear by Jacqueline McQuade. Teddy Bear is ready for his first day at preschool and at the end of the day he can hardly wait to get home to share his day with his cat.

Books About Sharing

Pat-a-Cake by Tony Kenyon. A toddler learns the fun of playing with someone else, and asks the baker for a cake to share with her baby sister.

Whoops! by Louise Batchelor. Two toddlers celebrate a birthday with their mothers while learning to share and use the words they know and enjoy.

Mine! by Miriam Cohen. Backpack Baby shows the possessions that belong to him that he is carrying on his walk. When he eats his pretzel he is very happy to share with his father.

Will I Have a Friend? by Miriam Cohen. Illustrated by Lillian Hoban. Jim is starting school, his very first day of kindergarten. His concerns about finding a friend are soon forgotten.

Sharing by Taro Gomi. Two little girls who are very good friends find interesting ways to divide things into equal parts to share.

Books About Naptime

If You Were My Bunny by Kate McMullan. Illustrated by David McPhail. Loving lullabies to baby animals can be sung to common tunes. The final song is from a mama to her baby.

No Nap by Eve Bunting. It's Susie's naptime, but Susie isn't tired. "No nap," she says. So dad makes his own plans to tire Susie out. A fresh and humorous approach to naptime.

Goodnight Moon by Margaret Wise Brown. A classic among books for young children. This is a perfect book to read before nap or bedtime.

Max's Bedtime by Rosemary Wells. Max can't go to sleep. Ruby tries everything but Max wants his red elephant. A humorous ending as Max falls out of bed and finds the elephant, and Ruby falls into his bed, exhausted from trying to get him to sleep.

Baby's Goodnight Book by Kay Chorao. This is a Lap Library book in sturdy board format. A beautifully illustrated collection of favorite lullabies for nap or bedtime.

The Napping House by Audrey and Don Wood. "There is a house, a napping house, where everyone is sleeping." An infectious, humorous, cumulative rhyming story. Children will giggle and chuckle all the way to bed. The board edition is perfect for toddlers to hold.

The Going to Bed Book by Sandra Boynton. For little ones reluctant to go to bed, sometimes a silly book is just the thing. Sandra Boynton is the queen of silly books and toddlers love them!

Index

A

Accidents, 104–105, 113
Afternoon, 120–121, 135
    fun box, 135
All about us books, 60, 63
Aprons, 121
Art activities, 99–100
Attendance cards, 75, 83

B

Baby traps, 149
Backpacks, 50
Backrubs, 53, 117
Bad-weather days, 124–126, 134
    fun box, 126, 135
Balancing, 49
Balls, 46, 84, 121, 125, 149, 151, 154
Baskets, 64, 74, 97, 116, 150
    laundry, 93, 150–151
Beanie Babies®, 135
Behavior transitions, 121–123
Benches, 151
Bibs, 114
Binders, 21, 63, 67
Blankets, 44–45, 50, 53, 68, 97, 115, 120, 125, 129, 148–149, 153
    doll, 55
Blocks, 151
Boats, 154
Body language, 144
Bolsters, 149
Book corner, 97–98
Books, 64, 98, 116–117, 119, 121, 130, 151
    about cleaning up, 94–95
    about friendship, 84–85, 158–159
    about hand washing, 111
    about naptime, 118–119, 159–160
    about security objects, 70, 157
    about separation, 68, 157
    about sharing, 88, 91, 159
    about toilet learning, 105
    "All About Us," 60, 63
    goodbye, 28
    homemade, 18, 27–28, 60, 63, 65, 67, 85, 88, 94–95, 111
    limiting number of, 98
    mommy comes back, 67
    moving up, 27–28
    respecting, 98
    sensory, 126, 135
Bouncing chairs, 149
Boxes, 65, 74–75, 121, 125, 148, 150
    bad-weather fun, 126, 135
    storage, 92
    treasure, 140
Briefcases, 66
Bubbles, 81
Buckets, 89
Butcher paper, 90

C

Cameras, 21, 27, 63, 67, 73, 85, 88, 94, 111
Canopies, 153
Capes, 107
Cardboard, 150
    blocks, 151
Caregivers
    as co-players, 79
    as social directors, 112
    biography, 21–22
    encouraging friendships, 83
    primary, 22–23, 29–30, 53, 101, 138–139
Carpet squares, 95
Carriages, 50
Cars, 89, 151
Carts, 94
Cassette players, 93
Cassette tapes, 66, 135
CD players, 93
CDs, 135
Cell phones, 65
Center transitions, 17–31
    continuity of care, 23–24
    entering childcare, 17–22
    from infant room to toddler room, 24–27
    from toddler room to preschool, 27–28
    leaving the program, 28–29
    primary caregivers, 22–23
    staff changes, 30–31
    staff transitions, 29–30
    weekend-to-Monday, 31
Chairs, 113, 125, 149
Changing tables, 156
Chenille stems, 121
Child development. See also Developmental notes
    crawling, 49, 154
    matching, 15
    mobility, 48, 154
    sitting, 48–49
    transitions, 48–50
    walking, 49–50, 154
Choices, 78, 101
Circle time, 90, 95–97
    dismissal, 96
    games, 84
    gathering song, 96
    rituals, 96
    shy puppet, 97

starting, 95
treasure box, 97
Class visits, 26, 28
Clay, 77, 126, 150
Cleanup time
after meals, 113
after snack, 76
books about, 94–95
infants, 46–47, 55
inspection train, 95
music, 93
outside, 107
pet puppets, 78
pet vacuum cleaner, 95
sorting game, 93–94
toddlers, 92–95
Climbers, 125, 150
Climbing, 154
Clothes
dress-up, 107, 151
extra, 92, 104
Clothesline, 108
Coats, 66
putting on, 107
songs about, 108
Communicating
about changing routines, 57
at pick-up time, 56
nonverbally, 133–134
notes, 22
phone calls, 22
photos, 22
with parents, 18–22, 24–26, 30
Conflict resolution, 83, 121–123
Consistency, 11, 61
in daily transitions, 29
in infant routines, 30–31
in toddler schedules, 72–73
Construction paper, 95, 114
Contact paper, 81, 121
clear, 67, 77, 113–114, 149, 150
Containers, 44, 77, 126, 150
Continuity of care, 23–24
Cooking activities, 99–100
Cooking utensils, 151
Cooperation, 14
Cots, 115–117, 120
Couches, 149
Crawling, 49, 154

Crayons, 49, 89, 126
Cribs, 53
Cruising, 154
Crying
at morning separation, 60–61
at pick-up time, 56
during mealtime, 40–41
Cubbies, 27, 129, 140
labeling, 19, 61
Cultural issues
around toilet training, 105
Curtains, 151

D
Daily routines, 30
changes in, 57
importance of, 11
photographing for parents, 21
with infants, 33–34
with toddlers, 72–73
Developmental notes, 138–147
importance of, 9
language skills, 143–147
Developmental transitions, 48–50, 154
to crawling, 49, 154
to mobility, 48, 154
to sitting, 48–49
to walking, 49–50, 154
Diapering
after naptime, 120
before naptime, 115–116
hand massage, 43
infants, 42–43
toddlers, 100–101
washing hands ritual, 43, 101
Digital cameras, 19, 21, 63
Discipline strategies, 15, 122
Discovery bottles, 126
Dish towels, 55, 114
Dish tubs, 150
Distracting, 122, 141
Dividers, 149, 150
Doll beds, 55
Dolls, 55, 66, 126, 151
Dramatic play, 150–151
Drawing materials, 85
Dress-up clothes, 107, 151

E
Egocentrism, 143
Emotional friendship, 22–23
Empathy, 39, 61–62, 123
End of the day, 126–128
Entering childcare, 17–22
building rapport with parents, 20–22
early communications, 22
empathizing with parents, 19–20
gradual enrollment, 19
intake interview, 18
welcoming the family, 19
Eye contact, 145

F
Fabric, 126, 150, 153
Facial expression, 145
Families door board, 66
Family photo board, 38
Family photos, 65–66, 121
Fine motor play, 154
Fingerpaint, 90, 127
Fingerplays, 121
Flashlights, 125
Flexibility, 18
Floor time, 14, 48–50, 149, 154
"Flop and do," 14
Flow of activities, 11
Flowers, 154
Food coloring, 128
Friendship, 26
affecting play, 82–83
books about, 84–85, 158–159
emotional, 22–23
empathetic friends, 64
encouraging, 83
forming, 82
groups, 84
importance of, 83–84
toddlers, 62, 82–85

G

Games
    can you find this? 79
    family-matching, 65
    follow the leader, 81
    interactive, 46
    noisy, 125
    parachute, 125
    peek-a-boo, 46
    problem hat, 135
    ring around the rosie, 84
    sorting, 93–94
General principles, 11–15
    consistency, 11
    cooperation, 14
    flop and do, 14
    importance of, 9
    making space work, 12
    matching children's development, 15
    nonverbal signals, 13
    pet puppets, 13–14
    preparation, 12
    re-entry, 15
    rehearsals, 13
    rituals, 12
Goodbye books, 28
Goodbye rituals, 61
    infants, 37, 39
    pretend play, 66–67
    toddlers, 128–132
Gradual enrollment, 19, 35, 60
Greeting children, 29, 31
    infants, 35–39
    toddlers, 60–68
Grooming time, 127
Gross motor play, 27, 154
Gym mats, 125
Gym time, 124

H

Hand massage, 43, 111
Hand washing, 43, 101, 104
    after meals, 113
    books about, 111
    soap gloves, 111
    toddlers, 110–111
Handouts, 20–21
Hats, 51, 70, 97, 107, 135

Health/safety issues, 155–156
Herding, 100

I

Imitation, 46, 84, 142
Independence, 110, 139
Indoor/outdoor carpeting, 153
Infant carriers, 50
Infant room
    child's view on leaving, 26–27
    leaving, 24–27
    moving up book, 27
Infant seats, 149
Infants
    daily transitions with, 33–57
    defined, 7
    developmental transitions, 58–50
    diapering, 42–43
    feeding, 40–42, 134
    going outside, 50–52
    individualized schedules, 33–34
    morning separation, 35–39
    pick-up time, 55–56
    playtime, 43–47
    routine changes, 57
    singing to, 38
    sleeping, 52–55
Inspection train, 95
Intake interviews, 18, 60–61
Interactive games, 46
Intonation, 145

K

Kitchen
    timers, 90–91
    utensils, 126

L

Labels, 19
Laminate, 63, 65, 67, 73, 75, 81, 95, 100, 150
Language skills, 143–147
    modeling, 146
    nonverbal, 144–145
    speaking "motherese," 146–147
Laundry baskets, 93, 150–151
Learning environments, 12, 148–152
    expanding play area, 150–151
    outdoors, 153–156

parent area, 151–152
    play area, 148–151
Leaving the program, 28–29
Legos®, 89, 126
Lending library, 152
Lights
    after nap, 120
    at pick-up time, 55
    dimming, 53, 117
    flashlights, 125
    patterns, 153
Listening cards, 109
Loose-leaf binders, 67
Lost-and-found spot, 152
Loveseats, 149
Lovey parties, 70
Lunchboxes, 66

M

Magnet boards, 121
Magnetic self-stick backing, 121
Magnetic strips, 63, 75
Manipulatives, 126
Masking tape, 121
Matching children's development, 15
Mats, 116, 120
Meal times
    bibs, 114
    infants, 40–42, 134
    preparing for, 40
    self-feeding, 41–42
    table-setting templates, 114
    toddlers, 112–114
Mirrors, 127, 150–151
Mobility, 48, 154
Modeling, 45, 122
    language skills, 146
"Mommy comes back" books, 67
Morning gathering time, 73–75
    taking attendance, 74–75
Morning separation
    anxiety, 139
    books about, 68, 157
    bye-bye ritual, 37, 39
    comforting, 38
    family photo board, 38
    infants, 35–39
    toddlers, 60–68
    welcome ritual, 37
    when parents can't leave, 39

Motherese, 146–147
Moving up book, 27–28
Music boxes, 121

N

Nametags, 18
Naptime
    books about, 118–119, 159–160
    children who don't nap, 119
    infants, 52–55
    lullabies, 52, 54
    magic sleep spray, 118
    pretending, 55
    toddlers, 115–120
    transitioning to, 53–54, 115–116
    waking up, 54, 119–120
    winding down, 52
Needles, 114
Newsletters, 19
Nonverbal communication, 133–134, 143–145
Nonverbal signals, 13, 116–117
Notes to parents, 22, 26, 129
Novelty, 140

O

Oppositional behavior, 59
    at pick-up time, 130–131
    during diapering, 101
    tantrums, 15, 123–124, 143
Organization, 77
Our day story, 128
Outdoor time, 89, 91
    coat trick, 107
    coming back inside, 52
    diapering, 156
    fine motor play, 154
    going for rides, 51–52
    gross motor play, 154
    infants, 50–52
    learning environments, 153–156
    preparing for, 51
    safety/health issues, 155–156
    sensory play, 153–154
    songs about, 108
    toddlers, 105–109
Overheating, 155
Overstimulation, 44, 122

P

Padded mats, 150
Paint, 94
    fingerpaint, 90, 127
    tempera, 127
Paintbrushes, 89
Pans, 106
Pantyhose, 110, 125
Paper, 21, 27, 67, 81
Paper cups, 51, 107, 155
Parachutes, 125
Parallel play, 15, 79, 82, 106
Parent board, 19, 22, 55, 129, 151
Parents
    area, 151–152
    building rapport with, 20–22
    consistent pick-up times, 128
    cooperating on toilet learning, 102–103
    early communications with, 22, 34
    empathizing with, 19–20, 25, 39
    getting to know staff, 30
    gradual enrollment process, 19
    greeting at pick-up time, 56, 129–130
    grief at leaving child, 20
    intake interview, 18
    involving in staff hiring, 30
    involving in transition decisions, 28
    letting know about staff changes, 30
    supporting during move to toddler room, 24–26
    talking about changing routines, 57
    visits by, 20–21
    welcoming, 19
    who can't leave, 39
Peek-a-boo, 46
Pegboards, 151
Pegs, 89, 151
Pens, 67
Pet puppets, 13–14, 74, 78, 88–92, 97, 117–118
Pet vacuum cleaner, 95
Phone calls, 22
Photo albums, 18, 65, 85, 88, 94, 111

Photographs, 21–22, 27, 55–56, 63, 65–66, 73, 75, 79, 81, 92, 95, 100, 113, 121, 129, 150–151
Pick-up time
    goodbye song, 131
    greeting parents, 56
    infants, 55–56
    oppositional behavior, 130–131
    toddlers, 128–132
    when children cry, 56
Picture seats, 95
Pillows, 95, 123, 149
Pipe cleaners, 121
Planning, 142
Plastic bags, 51, 107
    zippered, 27, 65, 85, 88, 94, 111, 127–128
Plastic bottles, 126
Plastic bowls, 126
Plastic cubes, 50
Platforms, 149
Play area, 148–151
    expanding for toddlers, 150–151
    nooks and crannies, 148–149
    organizing, 149–150
Play time
    adult's role, 46
    cleaning up, 46–47
    entering the play area, 44–45
    infants, 43–47
    play entry skills, 79–81
    playing with others, 45–46
    preparing for, 44
    stopping play, 47
    switching toys, 45
    toddlers, 77–81
    transitioning into, 77–79
Playdough, 77, 119, 150
Plexiglas, 153
Poem
    "What Do You See in the Sky?" 109
Poster board, 27, 66, 75
Posters, 151
Pounding benches, 151
Predictability, 139
Pre-enrollment, 35
Preschool, 27–28

Primary caregivers, 22–23, 29–30, 138–139
 at naptime, 53
 diapering, 101
 overlapping, 30–31
Printers, 21, 63
Problem hat game, 135
Promoting from within, 30
Pull toys, 151
Pulling up, 49–50
Puppets, 12–14, 74, 78, 88–91, 92, 117–118
 shy, 97
Push baskets, 154
Push toys, 151
Puzzles, 119, 126, 151

Q
Questions, 18

R
Ramps, 149
Recorded music
 classical, 52, 56
 parents singing, 66
 peppy, 93
 soft, 117
Redirecting, 122
Re-entry, 15, 124
Rehearsals, 13
Repetition, 142
Report binders, 63
Riding toys, 91, 125, 150
Rituals
 circle time, 96
 goodbye, 37, 39, 61, 66–67, 128–132
 hand washing, 43, 101, 104, 110–111
 importance of, 12
 outdoors, 156
 training, 134
 welcome, 37, 61
Rocking boats, 150
Rocks, 153
Routines. *See* Daily routines
Rubber tires, 153
Rugs, 90, 149

S
Safety notes, 51, 154
 outdoors, 155–156
Sand, 126
Sand play, 154
Saying goodbye, 28–29
 infants, 37, 39
 toddlers, 61, 66–67
Schedules
 for toddlers, 72–73
 individualized for infants, 33–34
 toilet learning, 104
 written, 34
Security objects, 117, 129, 140
 books about, 70, 157
 infants, 53
 toddlers, 68–71
Security, 138
 in daily routines, 11
Self-confidence, 8
Self-esteem, 8
 friendship and, 83–84
Self-feeding, 41–42
Sensory books, 126, 135
Sensory play, 15, 77, 81, 120, 126
 outdoors, 153–154
Separation. *See* Morning separation
Sewing, 27
Shaker bottles, 121
Shape boxes, 151
Sharing, 86–91
 books about, 88, 91, 159
Shaving cream, 81, 128
Sheets, 115, 149
Shelves, 151
Shoe bags, 150
Shoeboxes, 126, 150
Shopping bags, 150
Sitting up, 48–49
Slides, 125
Small groups, 26, 121
Smells, 154
Smocks, 150
Snack time, 75–76
 cleanup, 76
 come-and-go, 76
 singing at, 76
 traditional, 76

Snacks, 70, 120
 juice, 56, 126
Soap, 110–111
 gloves, 101, 111
Social groups, 45
Social influence, 141–142
Social skills
 conflict resolution, 83, 121–123
 friendship, 82–85
 play entry, 79–81
 sharing, 86–91
 taking turns, 86–91, 100
Solitary play, 45–46, 82
Songs, 9, 12, 38
 "Cleanup Song," 93
 "Come to the Table," 42, 76
 "Comfort Song," 38
 "Copy Me," 81
 "Gathering Song," 74, 96
 "Get on the Train," 109
 "Going Outside," 51, 108
 "Goodbye Song," 131
 "Greeting Song," 74
 "I'm Taking Care of You," 64
 "Lovey Song," 70
 lullabies, 52, 54
 "Putting on Coats," 108
 "Read Me a Story," 98
 "This Is the Way We Wash Our Hands," 43, 110
 transition, 135
 "The Wheels on the Bus," 125
Sounds, 153
Special equipment, 125
Sponges, 92, 154
Stacking cups, 151
Stacking rings, 151
Staff
 changes, 30–31
 daily transitions, 29–30
 ratios, 156
 training, 133–135
 transitions, 29–30
Starting over, 122–123
Stocking balls, 125
Story hats, 97
Story props, 99
Story time, 97–100
Streamers, 153

Stretching, 125
Strollers, 51
Stuffed animals, 53, 66, 68, 98, 116, 126, 129, 135, 149
Swings, 149, 155

T
Tables, 148
Table-setting templates, 114
Taking turns, 86–91, 100
Tantrums, 15, 123–124, 143
Tape recorders, 66
Teamwork, 50, 72, 115
Techniques, 11–15
    consistency, 11
    enticement, 14
    "flop and do," 14
    importance of, 9
    making space work, 12
    matching children's development, 15
    nonverbal signals, 13
    pet puppets, 13–14
    preparation, 12
    re-entry, 15, 124
    rehearsals, 13
    rituals, 12
Telegraphic speech, 146
Telephones, 65, 151
Textures, 153
Time awareness, 140–141
Time out, 15
Toddler room
    child's view on entering, 26–27
    leaving, 27–28
    "moving up" book, 27
    transitioning to, 24–27
Toddlers
    afternoons, 120–121
    bad-weather day activities, 124–125
    behavior transitions, 121–123
    circle time, 95–97
    cleanup time, 92–95
    daily transitions with, 59–132
    defined, 7
    diapering, 100–101
    end of the day, 126–128
    friendships, 82–85

    gross motor skills, 27
    hand washing, 110–111
    mealtimes, 112–114
    morning gathering time, 73–75
    morning separation, 60–68
    moving to other activities, 86
    moving to preschool, 27–28
    moving to toddler room, 24–27
    naptime, 115–120
    outside time, 105–109
    pick-up time, 128–132
    play area for, 150–151
    play entry skills, 79–81
    playtime, 77–79
    setting daily schedules, 72–73
    sharing, 86–91
    snack time, 75–76
    story time, 97–100
    taking turns, 86–91
    tantrums, 123–124
    toilet learning, 102–105
    transitional objects, 68–71
Toileting
    accidents, 104–105
    after naptime, 120
    before naptime, 115–116
    books about, 105
    cooperating with parents, 102–103
    cultural issues around, 105
    during outdoor time, 107
    learning, 102–105
    managing, 104
    signs of readiness, 103
Tote bags, 51
Tote bins, 150
Toys, 62, 151
    duplicating, 79, 87
    highlighting, 78, 120
    limiting number of, 86
    providing access, 44
    rotating, 150
    storing, 149
    switching, 45
Toy shelves, 149
Trains, 125
Transitional objects. *See* Security objects

Transitions
    behavior, 121–123
    between play activities, 86
    center, 17–31
    continuity of care, 23–24
    defined, 7
    developmental, 48–50, 154
    end of the day, 126–128
    entering childcare, 17–22
    from infant room to toddler room, 24–27
    from toddler room to preschool, 27–28
    leaving the program, 28–29
    morning gathering time, 73–75
    morning separation, 35–39, 60–68
    naptime, 52–55, 115–120
    pick-up time, 55–56, 128–132
    primary caregivers, 22–23
    staff changes, 30–31
    staff training for, 133–135
    staff transitions, 29–30
    toileting, 102–105, 107, 115–116, 120
    waking up, 54, 119–129
    weekend-to-Monday, 31
Treasure box, 140
Tubs, 89
Tummy time. *See* Floor time
Tunnels, 125, 150

U
Underpants, 104
Unit blocks, 151

V
Vacuum cleaners, 94
Vinyl-covered foam blocks, 151
Vocabulary, 8
Voice tone, 144

W
Wading pools, 149, 155
Wagons, 51, 94, 154
Waiting, 106, 121, 134
Waking up
    infants, 54–55
    toddlers, 119–120

Walkers, 149

Walking, 49–50, 124

Walking ropes, 13, 108, 124

Washcloths, 113, 126–127

Wastebaskets, 76

Water, 51, 89, 111, 123, 126

Water coolers, 107, 155

Water play, 106, 154

Water toys, 154

Weekend-to-Monday transitions, 31

Welcome rituals, 37, 61

Welcoming children. *See* Greeting children

Wet wipes, 51, 107

Wheel toys, 154

Whispering, 125

Wind chimes, 153

Wind socks, 153

Window boxes, 154

Wooden blocks, 151

Wooden cubes, 50

Z

Zippered plastic bags, 27, 65, 85, 88, 94, 111, 127–128